ALASKA:
The Big Land

ALASKA:
The Big Land

By BEN ADAMS

HILL AND WANG · NEW YORK

Copyright © 1959 by Hill and Wang, Inc.
Library of Congress Catalog Card Number: 59–8779
Manufactured in the United States of America

Acknowledgments

The poem on pp. 31–32 is reprinted by permission of Dodd, Mead & Company from *The Collected Poems of Robert Service*. Copyright 1917, 1945 by Robert Service.

For the photographs reproduced here by permission, the author extends thanks to Alaska Coastal Airlines for the pictures on pages 42, 138, 156, 171, and 175; Alaska Department of Agriculture for those on pages 126, 132, and 133; Alaska Housing Authority, pages 135, 137, 158, 159, 161, 181, and the drawings by George Ahgupuk on pages 5, 6, 27, 44, 78, and 124; Alaska Lumber & Pulp Company, page 56; Alaska Native Service, page 153; Alaska Railroad, pages 88, 89, 102, 103, 127, 178, 180, and 184; Alaska Rural Rehabilitation, pages 90 and 91; Alaska Visitors Association, pages iii, 7, 10, 11, 13, 19, 23, 33 (bottom), 37, 43, 57, 62, 63, 64, 65, 66, 67, 74, 75, 76, 77, 79, 80, 81, 95, 101, 110, 130, 131, 134, 139, 143, 144, 146, 148, 149, 155, 164, 165, 167, 168, 169, 170, 173, 174, 179, 186, 187, 188, 190, 191, 194, and 195; E. A. Hegg, photographer, lent by Nome Museum, pages 33 (top), and 34; Ketchikan Pulp Company, page 121; Mt. Edgecumbe School students, page 73; Northwest Orient Airlines, pages 136, 142, 145, 166, 177, 182, 183, 192, and 193; U.S. Army, pages 47, 49, 50, 51, 52, 53, 54, 60, 115, and 129; U.S. Bureau of Indian Affairs, Dept. of Interior, page 189; U.S. Bureau of Mines, Dept. of Interior, pages 117 and 118; U.S. Coast Guard, pages 154 and 160; U.S. Department of Interior, pages 14 and 116; U.S. Fish & Wildlife Service, Dept. of Interior, pages 104, 105, 106, and 151; U.S. Forest Service, Dept. of Agriculture, pages 9, 61, 70, 108, 122, 157, 172, 176, and 185; U.S. Navy, page 46; Wein Alaska Airlines, page 68; Wickersham Collection, pages 29, 30, 31, 32, 35, 36, 85, 87, and 109.

The map on page 2 is reproduced by permission of Rand McNally & Company.

The photographs on the jacket of the cloth-bound edition and the cover of the paperback edition are used with the following permissions: front, left and right, Alaska Visitors Association, center, U.S. Forest Service; back, left column top to bottom, U.S. Air Force, U.S. Fish & Wildlife Service, Alaska Visitors Association; and back jacket, right column, Alaska Visitors Association.

Contents

ALASKA:
The Big Land

ALASKA

Polyconic Projection
SCALE 1 : 23,800,000   1 Inch = 375 Statute Miles

Statute Miles 50 25 0   50   100   150   200   250
Kilometers 50 0   100   200   300

1: The Hardy Ice Worm

It happened at the end of the last century in the gold rush town of Dawson in Yukon Territory. A penniless but resourceful writer named E. H. White was having a little trouble filling the regular column he did for the *Klondike Nugget.* So he made himself up a yarn about a night when blue snow fell and the temperature dropped to 70° below. That night, he said, the ice worms came to the surface in search of some real cold and chirped madly, keeping the residents awake.

White's real news stories never attracted much attention. But this whopper made headlines around the world. Scientists solemnly discussed the genus Alaska ice worm. White hastily explained that it was all a hoax. But eager editors accused him of suppressing information, insisted on details. So he elaborated his yarn. For a time the ice worm was one of the more popular forms of Alaskan animal life. Saloonkeepers dished up ice-worm cocktails to the gullible, with a few shreds of spaghetti frozen into the ice.

The ice worm became a part of Alaska folk lore. Everybody was willing to believe anything about Alaska—including such "minor" inaccuracies as putting the Canadian Yukon in Alaska. Any story was accepted as long as it was fantastic enough and had generous trimmings of snow, ice and −70° weather.

The truth had harder sledding. As long ago as 1884, Hubert

Howe Bancroft, the historian of the old West, wrote in his *History of Alaska:* "It is not always and altogether that cold and desolate region which sometimes has been pictured, and which from its position we might expect. Its configuration and climate are exceedingly varied. The southern seaboard is comparatively mild and hospitable; the northern frigid and inhospitable." But nobody believed him.

Almost seventy-five years after Bancroft, United States senators making a last-ditch stand against statehood assured their colleagues in the world's greatest deliberative body that Alaska was too cold and barren for human habitation. But at long last, the facts caught up with fiction. The senators were more impressed with the facts.

Alaska is easily our richest state in terms of natural resources. There is still plenty of gold around, although nobody seems to want it right now. What is more important, Alaska has oil, copper, coal, iron ore, nickel, uranium, chrome, and many other minerals. The water power of mighty streams waits to be harnessed. There are limitless forests with fine timber, and countless fish in the rivers and in the sea.

Alaska is by far the biggest state in the union. There are 586,-400 square miles of it, twice the size of Texas, one fifth the size of the entire United States. It is farther from Ketchikan, in southeastern Alaska, to Attu, westernmost of the Aleutian Islands, than it is from New York to San Francisco. You hardly step off the plane before you hear the current definition of claustrophobia—an Alaskan in Texas.

Alaska has the highest mountain in North America, Mount McKinley in south-central Alaska, rising 20,320 feet almost straight up. It has the biggest glaciers, one of them in the Alaskan "panhandle," as big as Rhode Island. It has the longest coast line, more than enough to circle the globe. It has the most abundant wild life, even buffalo roaming the range.

Alaska can become America's greatest treasure house of scarce raw materials—and its most spectacular vacation land.

Centuries ago the Aleut islanders, paddling over in their canoes to the mainland, looked up in awe and called it Al-ay-ek-sa—

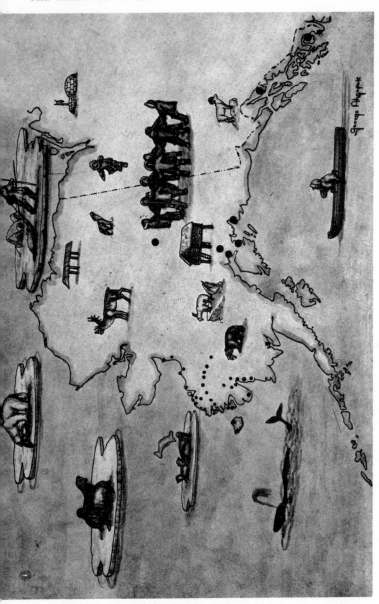

Picture map of Alaska by the Eskimo artist, George Ahgupuk

From across the waters came the Eskimo

meaning the great land or the big land. In Aleut language it is spelled: Alaxsxaq. That is how it got its name, and it is still overwhelming. Alaska is still the biggest, the richest, the most spectacular.

Americans tend to think of all Alaska as Polar or at least Arctic. Not all who created the impression of Alaska as a frozen wasteland were pure in heart, but most have been innocent enough. Writers of novels, adventure stories, and reminiscences about Alaska have stressed the romantic and the extreme. After all, who would want to write about a warm summer day in Fairbanks —or read about it?

Sometimes Alaskans are themselves responsible for misconceptions. A bright promoter got the idea of calling a little village on the outskirts of Fairbanks "North Pole—The Home of Santa Claus." This has been good for business; yet Fairbanks is about 120 miles south of the Arctic Circle, and more hundreds of miles south of the North Pole. Besides, Alaskans who have been the butt of so many bad jokes can't help kidding the cheechako outsider. A bartender at a lodge about half way between Anchorage and Fairbanks will proudly show you the downstairs trophy room —including, among the mooseheads and the salmon, an "Alaska fur fish." This rare specimen, with a fine coat of muskrat, is, of course, a close cousin of the ice worm.

But mostly Alaska has been a victim of its own violent con-

Alaska cows are unimpressed by rugged mountains

trasts. Alaska's weather does get as cold as 78° below—but it also gets as hot as 100° and usually in the same places. It does have short winter days—but it also has long summer days. It does have thousands of miles of barren tundra—but it also has great forests with first-rate timber and about a million acres of good agricultural land. It does have awesome glaciers—but you can also see cows grazing peacefully within sight of some of those glaciers. Somehow, it is only the formidable, the uninhabitable, the unconquerable aspects of Alaska that become known and remembered, while the great variety in its climate and terrain is forgotten.

Actually, three-fourths of Alaska is in the North Temperate Zone. It is as near, and as far from, the North Pole as Scotland, Norway, Finland, and Sweden; and much of its weather is about the same. Generalizations about Alaska weather, as about almost everything else in Alaska, are misleading. The temperature fluctuates sharply with the seasons, and there are big differences between the various areas. Juneau, the capital, has an average mean temperature in February of 30°, almost identical with that of New York City, whereas Fairbanks in the same month has an average of −1.6°.

Alaska is a great peninsula jutting out from the northwestern tip of the North American continent. We sometimes forget that it juts out to the west more than to the north. It is part of the North Pacific area even more than of the Arctic Ocean which borders it in the north. All of Alaska is west of the rest of the United States, some of it west of the Hawaiian Islands. The warm Japan current moderates the weather along the coast.

It is a queerly shaped peninsula. You can picture it perhaps as a crudely made wheelbarrow with two long handles fanning out from the front. The body of the wheelbarrow runs 900 miles at its longest, 800 miles across at its widest. One handle fans out to the east, the other—even longer—spreads far to the west toward Asia and includes the Aleutian Islands.

Alaska's geography and climate are so varied that authorities divide it up into anywhere from three to ten areas. Perhaps four will be sufficient for most purposes.

Southeast Alaska is the handle of the wheelbarrow closer to the United States and bordering on British Columbia. Only a thin strip of coast connects it with the mainland. Most of it is a maze of islands green with forests of spruce and hemlock and blue with countless channels and inlets. The average temperature here is about the same as Philadelphia. In summer the weather reminds you of Seattle and Portland, pleasant but rainy. July temperatures in the two big southeast cities of Ketchikan and Juneau run in the middle fifties, although it sometimes gets pretty hot. The January temperature is about the same as that in Maryland and southern Illinois. In fact, the southeast is so far from an Arctic waste that hardy sourdoughs refer to it a bit contemptuously as "the banana belt."

Western Alaska—a loose designation—is the vast Pacific coastal area west of the narrow strip of southeast Alaska. It is a coast ringed by great mountains, an extension of the Pacific moun-

A typical scene in Southeast Alaska, with the killer whale totem
in the foreground

tain system. Included in this general area are the Kenai Peninsula,
a sanctuary for moose and a happy hunting ground for oil; the
Matanuska Valley, Alaska's major agricultural center; Kodiak
Island, where the Russians first settled; the Bristol Bay fishing
communities; the sparsely settled Alaska Peninsula; and the long
string of Aleutian Islands. The center of this immense area is
Anchorage, Alaska's biggest and most important city. The climate
is generally temperate in Western Alaska, although it gets pretty
stormy in the Aleutians. The summer temperature in Anchorage is
about the same as in southeastern Alaska, but it gets colder in
the winter.

The Interior is the country considered the real Alaska by most

Horseshoe Lake in Mount McKinley National Park

of the old-timers. It sprawls north from the Alaska Range to the Yukon Valley, from the Canadian border west to the Bering Sea. Here is much of the old gold-mining country, country famed for hunting and trapping. There are forests and wooded areas, but the trees do not grow as big on the great interior plateau. Many rivers wind their way through grassy plains and tundras, the Kuskokwim, the Porcupine, the Tanana—and, of course, the Yukon which girdles the whole breadth of Alaska. Fairbanks is the metropolis of the Interior. Here the weather gets hot in the summer, as high as 99° in Fairbanks, and very cold in the long winter, as low as −66°.

The Arctic area lies between the Yukon Valley and the Arctic Ocean. Here is the real tundra, the rolling uplands and the im-

Eskimo girls take plane travel in stride

mense area of flat plain north of the Brooks Mountains. Down from the mountains toward the ocean is the Arctic prairie of surprisingly rich grassland. While northern Alaska is generally wild and uninhabited, there are even here considerable areas where vegetables will grow. Around Nome there are 176 different kinds of wild flowers in the summer—a fact which residents quickly call to your attention. Here the summers are cool, but the winters not quite as cold as the Interior farther south. Great winter storms, however, make the climate less bearable. Except for Nome, there are only scattered Eskimo villages in the Arctic, some fairly sizable.

Alaska can be gentle and rugged, the country green and lush or brown and desolate, the weather hot or cold or in between. Perhaps the most important thing to keep in mind is that Alaska is full of variety and contrast in geography, in climate, in everything else. Popular misconceptions that put a uniform tag on everything in Alaska are unfortunately not confined to the weather. They extend to the people and how they live.

Don't expect to see igloos in Alaska—at least not the ice-block igloos of the comic strips and cartoons. Most Eskimos now live in ordinary although inadequate wooden houses. The igloo is the traditional Eskimo house of sod with driftwood for a frame. At times igloos were built of snow blocks as a temporary shelter, but these were hardly the ordinary Eskimo dwelling place.

Contrary to widespread belief, most people in Alaska are not Eskimos. Alaska's population in 1958 was about 210,000. There were 16,000 Eskimos. In fact, Eskimos make up a little less than half of Alaska's native population. The others are 14,000 Indians who live in the southeast and in the interior, and 4,000 Aleuts who live in the extreme west of Alaska and on the Aleutian Islands.

Most of Alaska's natives speak English and have gone to school. Indeed, this is true of practically all of them except some of the older generation. Many have gone to college and have become teachers, plane pilots, skilled technicians for Army Arctic installations. It is true that in isolated Eskimo villages the whale hunt is still the big event of the year and that the women still slaughter and process the seal. But even there life is a strange mixture of new and old. Outboard motors are often attached to the Eskimo umiaks or open boats.

You find the same odd mixture almost everywhere in Alaska. There are many villages where the only means of transportation known to most of the people are dog-sled—and airplane. Even a number of sizable cities are inaccessible by road or railroad. But there is excellent plane service to even the most isolated villages. Planes are Alaska's buses and taxis. There is an Indian village near Anchorage with an old burying ground of little wooden houses for the possessions of the dead. Nearby is a $30,000,000 electric power plant. An ultra-modern pulp mill is being built in Sitka, only a few minutes' ride from a fine collection of old totem poles.

Fairbanks with the Chena River in the background

You could describe Fairbanks as a rugged frontier town with ramshackle old log cabins right off the main street and some tough bars. But that would be a half-truth. Fairbanks also has modern elevator apartment buildings, movie theaters, two TV stations, a good newspaper and a fine university which is the greatest pride of most Alaskans. Anchorage has a new, raw look about it. With its flat, wide streets you might mistake it for a midwestern farm town, uninteresting and unenterprising. But it is bustling with enterprise. It is also, surprisingly enough, the center of flourishing little theaters and quite a lively cultural movement.

Most Alaskans are town-dwellers, not trappers or hunters. And

Hydraulic gold operation in the Yukon River region

urban living in Alaska has most, although not all, of the modern conveniences. There are some inconveniences too. The cost of living is quite high. It can get quite cold in the winter, especially in Fairbanks. But for Alaskans there are compensations that outweigh all their problems and gripes. There is the fellowship of sharing in building a new country and a new life, the joys of beautiful scenery and outdoor living and a sense of opportunity—not perhaps an opportunity for getting rich quick from a sudden gold strike, but for making a better livelihood than is available elsewhere.

Say Alaska to most people on an association test, and they will probably answer gold, if not ice. Lots of gold was taken out of Alaska's streams and beaches and hills—more than $700,000,000 of it over the years. Gold was also the source of another industry besides mining. Jack London never made any money panning gold, but he struck rich pay dirt writing about it. From the gold rush sprang the myths and legends of the Old Yukon, of the giants who battled with nature and each other, of fortunes made and lost on the turn of a card. The writings of London, Rex Beach, and Robert Service were based on reality. But they also tended to give a romanticized picture of Alaska, singling out the most spectacular and unusual in man and nature.

Fish are, of course, less romantic than gold. But as a dollar and cents proposition, the value of the fish taken out of Alaska's waters has been three times as great as all the gold. The take from fish, mostly salmon, now runs to about $90,000,000 a year, while gold dribbles out in a mere trickle of some $8,000,000. Fish are still the basis of Alaska's biggest industry. But it is a sick industry —seasonal and with violent ups and downs; even the teeming salmon in Alaska's waters are not inexhaustible. Almost as much coal in dollar value is mined now as gold. But coal is considered potentially far more important. So is oil, which is generally considered the black gold of the future, the source of Alaska's next gold rush.

But Alaska's greatest resource is its people. Their average age is younger, their average schooling higher than in most of the U.S.A. They have a desire for education and self-betterment which includes all Alaskans, the native peoples and the whites alike. They are intensely civic-minded, taking pride in building up their communities and in contributing to the growth of the new state. They are as friendly and sociable and co-operative a group as you could hope to find. They are also rugged individualists, the largest collection of them extant. Alaskans have to have a dash of the pioneering spirit, of drive or dedication, and most of them do. They stick with it, too. Alaska's population is considerably more settled than it used to be. There are now thousands of second- and third-generation Alaskans, sons and daughters and grandsons and granddaughters of original pioneers.

Few people who see Alaska for themselves will question whether it was ready for statehood. It was objected that Alaska's population was small. But most territories had considerably smaller population when they were admitted to the Union. When Nevada became a state in 1864, the last census figures gave it a population of 6,857; in the 1950 Census, it barely topped the 160,000 mark.

Alaska's population is made of the same stuff that built the West. Statehood helped most territories grow, and it will do the same for Alaska, our forty-ninth state.

The remarkable thing is not that so few people came to Alaska and stayed, but that so many did. They had to overcome man-made obstacles as well as the hardships of living in pioneer country. Alaska was for decades the victim of official neglect. It was the target of both governmental and business discrimination. Its great wealth enriched few Alaskans but flowed to Seattle and New York City. It had to fight every inch of the way for each small measure of self-government it gained. It started fighting for statehood back in 1916.

Alaskans are sensitive about the misconceptions of Alaska as a barren land of snow and ice. They have had to pay for the long neglect by their fellow citizens, broken only by occasional redis-coveries of "Seward's Folly." Americans became aware of Alaska for the first time during the gold rush, then forgot about it in a few years. World War II rediscovered Alaska, helped lead to the growth in population and the development of Alaska's economy which have hastened statehood.

Now statehood—officially proclaimed on January 3, 1959—has again made millions of Americans conscious of Alaska. Ignorance of Alaska was perhaps once excusable; it was far away and hard to reach. But it no longer is: Ketchikan is only 2½ hours from Seattle by plane. Visitors to Alaska will not find ice worms, fur fish, and igloos there. But you will find some of the most beautiful country in the world, a wonderful place to vacation, an important defense outpost, and a land rich in resources and opportunity. Alaskans are hoping that this rediscovery will be permanent.

2: Russian Bear and Buzzard's Beak

Alaska is a young, bustling state with its eyes on the future. It is also a place in which you are constantly reminded of the past. An old-timer in Juneau is liable to pull out a handsome Russian book dating back some hundred years and show you the color plates of Czars and Empresses in full regalia who paved the way for the settlement of Alaska. Place names: Baranof Island, St. Michael, Resurrection Bay, and occasional Greek Orthodox churches with their Greek cupolas remind you of the Russian past. Old saloons try to capitalize on the relics and the faded memories of the gold-rush days, and there are still old prospectors around who will tell you tales by the hour of the Klondike strike and the golden beaches at Nome. A brisk young banker in Anchorage, explaining how statehood will stimulate the growth of Alaska, may suddenly bang on the table with anger as he recalls the discriminations and liabilities of absentee domination which burdened Alaska in the past. History seems part of the present here—because Alaska is only now beginning to emerge out of its past.

If you should visit Sitka, climb a little hill right off the main street near the water front. You will reach a flat elevation overlooking a necklace of wooded islands, strung like dark jade on a sparkling blue string of Pacific channels and inlets. You will see there a rusted cannon with an imperial Russian crest, mounted on heavy unpainted boards. A few feet away you will see a flag pole and a brass plaque at the base with the barely decipherable inscription: "On this site Oct. 18, 1867 the American flag was raised on the territory of Alaska by members of company of Company E 9th Infantry United States Army."

Here an era ended, and an era began. Here once stood the big wooded home of Alexander Andreyevich Baranof who ruled Alaska for twenty years with an iron hand and even reached out to California and the Hawaiian Islands. The house was called Baranof's Castle, but everything was a bit grandiose in those days. Here the one-time Russian dream of empire in the new world died in a sad ceremony on the bright and sunny afternoon of that October day recorded on the plaque.

Stiffly at attention stood 100 Russian troops and 200 American soldiers, marines, and sailors while a commissioner of the Imperial Russian Government announced that Alaska was being turned over to the United States. Guns boomed alternately from Russian and American warships. Prince Maksoutoff, the last Russian governor of Alaska, gave the signal for the Russian flag to be lowered. The story goes that the flag got fouled in the ropes and would not come down. A man had to be sent aloft; he tore the flag down and flung it on the damp earth. The Princess, looking out of her window, wept.

A small, neglected graveyard only a short distance away suggests that there was personal tragedy here as well as the long sweep of history. Here is the grave of a Russian lieutenant who died at the age of 30 in 1848. What dreams of conquest did he dream? And how did he die? Was it of sickness? Or in fighting with the hostile Indians? "Peace be to your dust," says the inscription. Here is a stone to "our dearly beloved son Philip Kashavaroff," who died at the age of two in 1868, his brief life spanning the passing of the old and the coming of the new.

It all started with Peter the Great of Russia in the early eighteenth century. Peter looked westward for new ideas and able men who would help him modernize old Russia. He also looked east-

Main street of Sitka, the old Russian capital, with the old
Greek Orthodox Church in the background

ward to Siberia and Asia to expand his empire. He had heard in
Holland of the old quest of sailors and explorers for a northern
short cut between Europe and Asia. Perhaps he would find it by
going east.

In 1725, shortly before he died, Peter ordered Vitus Bering,
a Danish navigator, to build a couple of boats at Kamchatka and
then proceed north along the coast of Siberia to find out "where
it is joined to America." Then he was "to reach some city in
European possession, and to enquire what it is called, and to make
a note of it."

It was not that easy for Bering. The nearest European colonies
were thousands of miles away. Even to get started on his voyages
he and his men had to haul ship-building equipment across 5,000
miles of mountain and steppe. On his first trip Bering discovered
St. Lawrence Island, now part of Alaska, and concluded that the
Asiatic and American continents were separate rather than joined.

He was jeered on his return. Learned armchair geographers, consulting maps drawn from sailors' yarns and their own musings, determined that he could not possibly have been where he said he had been. He was given new and more elaborate instructions to establish a mail route to China and chart the entire coast of Siberia as well as the coast of North America south to Mexico.

For the next ten years Bering and his sailors explored the Siberian coast and the unknown lands to the east. In May 1741 the ice broke up and Bering undertook his last voyage. On July 16 he sighted a great snow-peaked mountain. Bering had found America. He was off the southeast coast of Alaska. It was St. Elias Day, and he called his mountain Mount St. Elias. But Bering was now an old man of 60, broken by years of hardship. He died on his return trip in a temporary shelter on what is now Bering Island, unhonored and unrecognized.

One of the men on Bering's ship was Georg Wilhelm Steller, a young German-born botanist. Before Bering sailed back, Steller won permission to land at the island of Kayak off the Alaska coast. In a few short hours, he collected many hitherto unknown birds and plants. One was a bird of bright blue plumage. Suddenly Steller recalled having seen a similar bird in a colored picture book by an Englishman on the natural history of the Carolinas and Florida. "This bird proved to me that we were really in America," Steller said later.

On the basis of his trip Steller described four hitherto unknown mammals, the sea cow, the sea lion, the sea otter, and the fur seal. The first two were marine curiosities. The last two changed the history of Alaska and the Pacific Coast. The survivors of Bering's crew brought back a cargo of furs, including the soft iridescent sea otter fur with its sprinkling of silver. The furs had almost the same impact in Siberia as the later discovery of gold in California and Alaska.

Fast on the heels of Bering came the *promyshlenniki,* the Russian equivalent of our frontiersmen. They were the hunters and trappers of Siberia, rugged, boisterous fellows who provided sable, marten, ermine, and beaver skins to the hard-drinking, sharp-trading Siberian merchants. The merchants sent the *promyshlen-*

niki east to Alaska on crude, flat-bottomed craft with a deck and a sail. Expedition followed expedition. The sea otter were relentlessly pursued. Their pelts were a great success in Russia, in Europe, and in China, where the fur was used at the imperial court to trim the robes of the mighty.

Companies were formed by merchants and traders and competed vigorously with each other. One of the richest and most aggressive of these merchants was Gregory Shelikof, who founded a settlement on Kodiak Island in 1784. But the Czarist government pressed Shelikof and his competitors to consolidate their interests in order to gain a monopoly on Alaska trade. This was the Russian-American Company formed in 1799. Baranof, who had been Shelikof's manager, was made directing head of the new firm, which was an arm of the Russian government much as the British trading companies had been of theirs. High Russian officials and nobles were put in high places in the company.

There was a reason for the Russian government's intervention in the Alaska game. Spain, England, and France were all showing considerable interest in the northwest coast of the continent. All three countries sponsored explorations in Alaskan waters, ostensibly for purposes of exploration. But the Russians were uneasy. The Spanish started making claims to territory in southern Alaska. Captain James Cook's British sailors sold sea otter skins in Canton. Later came the voyages of Captain Frederick William Beechey, the British explorer, who sailed up and down the coast of northwest Alaska and of the Canadian Arctic. It was necessary for the Russians to consolidate their territory, found permanent settlements, if they were to hold Alaska.

Besides, Russia had her dreams of a great empire in the North Pacific. A contemporary Soviet historian says that Alaska was to be the major base in a "grandiose plan of expansion" which would turn the North Pacific into "an inland sea." California was "to serve as an agricultural base for the Russian colonies in America." The Hawaiian Islands were to give Russia control of "all the seaborne trade with China."

For the first twenty years, the period during which Baranof was in charge, things went fairly well. The Aleuts were organized into great hunting parties, forced to provide hundreds of canoes full of men for the spring season. Plenty of *promyshlenniki,* the white hunters, were picked up in the taverns of Siberian towns, often shanghaied aboard ship or induced to sign long-term contracts while drunk. The sea otter were slaughtered by the thousands, the more plentiful fur seal by the hundreds of thousands. The company paid dividends.

Life was never easy for the Russians in Alaska. The Aleuts were by no means as docile as they have sometimes been pictured. The first *promyshlenniki* were merciless, often shooting down whole villages. Massacre Bay on Attu Island got its name from such an incident. As early as 1764 the Aleuts rose up in bloody retaliation. Many years later they sent a letter to Czar Paul I complaining of his representatives: "We receive them in friendly fashion, but they act like barbarians with us. They seize our wives and children as hostages. . . ." The Aleuts even sent a delegation to Paul. They were kindly received and given rich clothing. But somehow none of the delegates managed to reach home. The last two died mysteriously in Siberia just before their departure.

Finally the Aleuts were subdued. But the Thlinget Indians in the southeast—the Russians called them Kolosh—gave even more trouble. In 1801 they burned Baranof's fort at Sitka, and he had to rebuild. Baranof complained that they wore several coats of wooden armor "wherefore neither bullets nor bricks nor arrows nor pikes were powerful enough to defeat them." They also had guns provided, the Russians said resentfully, by rival British and Yankee traders. The Russians never really conquered the Thlinget. As late as 1855, the latter attacked Sitka.

Moreover, Baranof had trouble with the *promyshlenniki.* They felt that they were being cheated of their share of the pelts promised them by the company. They grew restive and resentful, especially during the idle winters. In 1809 they even organized a revolt against Baranof at Sitka which he ruthlessly put down.

But somehow Baranof managed to keep things under control. He was a hard driver, a successful manager. Washington Irving described him as "a rough, rugged, hard-drinking old Russian, somewhat of a soldier, somewhat of a trader; above all a boon

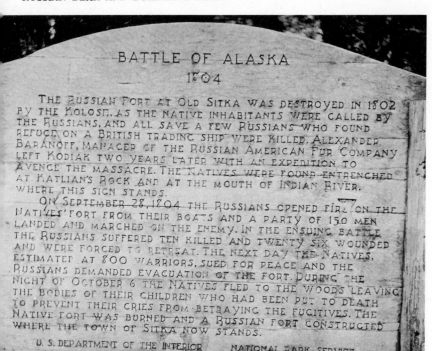

BATTLE OF ALASKA
1804

THE RUSSIAN FORT AT OLD SITKA WAS DESTROYED IN 1802 BY THE KOLOSH, AS THE NATIVE INHABITANTS WERE CALLED BY THE RUSSIANS, AND ALL SAVE A FEW RUSSIANS WHO FOUND REFUGE ON A BRITISH TRADING SHIP WERE KILLED. ALEXANDER BARANOFF, MANAGER OF THE RUSSIAN AMERICAN FUR COMPANY LEFT KODIAK TWO YEARS LATER WITH AN EXPEDITION TO AVENGE THE MASSACRE. THE NATIVES WERE FOUND ENTRENCHED AT KATLIAN'S ROCK AND AT THE MOUTH OF INDIAN RIVER, WHERE THIS SIGN STANDS.

ON SEPTEMBER 28, 1804 THE RUSSIANS OPENED FIRE ON THE NATIVES' FORT FROM THEIR BOATS AND A PARTY OF 150 MEN LANDED AND MARCHED ON THE ENEMY. IN THE ENSUING BATTLE THE RUSSIANS SUFFERED TEN KILLED AND TWENTY SIX WOUNDED AND WERE FORCED TO RETREAT. THE NEXT DAY THE NATIVES, ESTIMATED AT 800 WARRIORS, SUED FOR PEACE AND THE RUSSIANS DEMANDED EVACUATION OF THE FORT. DURING THE NIGHT OF OCTOBER 6 THE NATIVES FLED TO THE WOODS LEAVING THE BODIES OF THEIR CHILDREN WHO HAD BEEN PUT TO DEATH TO PREVENT THEIR CRIES FROM BETRAYING THE FUGITIVES. THE NATIVE FORT WAS BURNED AND A RUSSIAN FORT CONSTRUCTED WHERE THE TOWN OF SITKA NOW STANDS.

U. S. DEPARTMENT OF THE INTERIOR   NATIONAL PARK SERVICE

Plaque commemorating battles between the Russians and
the Thlingit Indians

companion of the old roystering school, with a strong cross of the bear." He encouraged the *promyshlenniki* to forget their troubles in wild dancing, drinking bouts, and promiscuous relations with the native women.

Baranof persisted. He had the California coast seeded with markers inscribed "Land Belonging to Russia." In 1812 he started the colony of Ross near San Francisco. A few years later he dispatched an adventurous doctor to Hawaii to start a colony there. But his venture did not last long. Yankee traders were already too well established, and they used their influence to have him driven out.

Particularly after Baranof's death in 1819, things started to worsen for the Russians. They aroused the enmity of both the British and the Americans. The two traditional foes buried the hatchet to meet the threat of Russian expansion in North America. Russia was one of the main targets of the Monroe Doctrine in 1823 which warned European powers to stop meddling in American affairs; and the British backed up the U.S. The Russians had to limit their territorial ambitions and make important concessions to both the British and the Americans. Then the Mexicans started giving them trouble at Fort Ross, and the Americans were beginning to crowd into California. The Russians finally sold their California colony to Captain John Sutter on whose farm gold was later discovered.

After a while, even the Russian holdings in Alaska became a liability. The Russian-American Company wasn't making any money and needed government subsidies to keep going. The sea otter had been slaughtered almost to extinction. The seal and other furs were becoming scarce. The Russians had been profligate in their practices, had ruined millions of skins in dyeing, burned millions of others to keep prices up. The British Hudson's Bay Company and John Jacob Astor's American trappers were giving them competition for the fur trade. Yankee sailors took over the whaling trade. The Russians had botched the job. They never penetrated the interior. They did virtually no farming. They did not touch Alaska's rich mineral resources. Besides, they became more interested in expansion in the Far East than in America.

It was hardly worth keeping Alaska, particularly since it seemed that they might have to fight Britain for it. The Hudson's Bay Company kept invading territory in Alaska claimed by Russia. There was even a clash between Russian warships and a British brig in southeast Alaska. After the Crimean War with Britain ended in 1856, the Russians started casting around for a way to get rid of Alaska. A new turn in international relations made the United States the logical buyer. The Americans were now having trouble with the British again and had become friendly with the Russians.

The United States clashed sharply with Britain over the Oregon-

Canadian border, and the slogan "Fifty-Four Forty or Fight" summed up American sentiment. During the Civil War, the British, tied by commercial relations to the Confederate South, were unfriendly to the Union. So were the French for that matter. Only the Russians seemed sympathetic. Freeing of the serfs by Czar Alexander II in 1861 and emancipation of the slaves by Lincoln in 1863 almost coincided. For a time there was a sentimental romance between the two countries.

An accident fanned the international love affair. Fearing that its navy was too weak to fight the British in another war, the Russian government in 1863 ordered its fleet to put into port in San Francisco and New York. Most Americans saw this as a demonstration of solidarity with the Union. There were glittering receptions for the gallant Russian officers. Toasts were downed "to Lincoln the Emancipator and Alexander the Liberator." When Grand Duke Alexis visited the United States in 1871, Oliver Wendell Holmes rhapsodized:

> Throbbing and warm are the hearts that remember
> Who was our friend when the world was our foe.

It was on this wave of good feeling that Secretary of State William H. Seward and Baron Edouard de Stoeckl, the Russian Minister in Washington, were able to consummate one of the world's bigger real estate deals.

Stoeckl was eager to sell. He had, in fact, conducted tentative discussions on the subject in Washington in 1860. But in 1866 he got a final go-ahead from St. Petersburg, which set a minimum price of $5,000,000.

Seward was just as eager to buy. He was an expansionist, seeking to build American power in the Pacific. He saw Alaska as a bridge between America and Asia. Two developments seemed helpful. With the co-operation of the Russian government, the Western Union Company had begun laying a telegraph line to Europe through Alaska and Siberia. The project was abandoned when the Atlantic cable was laid in 1866. But American engineers, surveying Alaska, had formed some idea of its possibilities. The other was an insistent demand by West Coast fishing interests for the right to fish in Alaskan waters. Seward took advantage of this issue. He presented the fishing problem to Stoeckl and hoped it would become an opening wedge for the purchase of Alaska.

Soon the two diplomats got down to the real issue. Seward offered $5,000,000 for Alaska. Stoeckl asked $7,000,000, and he quickly realized that he didn't have to compromise with such an anxious customer. He stood by his figure, and Seward eventually topped it by $200,000.

On the evening of March 29, 1867, Seward was playing whist with his family in his parlor when Stoeckl was announced.

"I have a dispatch, Mr. Seward, from my government by cable," said the Russian Minister. "The Emperor gives his consent to the cession. Tomorrow, if you like, I will come to the department, and we can enter upon the treaty."

"Why wait till tomorrow, Mr. Stoeckl?" said Seward, pushing away the whist table. "Let us make the treaty tonight."

The two men rushed to the State Department where the lights burned late all that night. At Seward's side was Senator Charles Sumner, chairman of the Senate Foreign Relations Committee and one of the few men in Washington who favored the purchase. By 4 A.M. the treaty was signed. Later that day President Andrew Johnson sent a brief special message to the Senate submitting "a treaty for the cession of Russian America."

Seward had acted quickly and secretly. Now came a violent reaction from Congress and the press. "Seward's Folly" and "Johnson's Polar Bear Garden" were among the milder epithets. A typical comment was a fictitious ad in the *New York Herald:*

CASH! CASH! CASH!—Cash paid for cast-off territory. Best price given for old colonies, North, or South. Any impoverished monarchs retiring from the colonization business may find a good purchaser by addressing W.H.S., Post Office, Washington, D.C.

Engineers who had been in Alaska for Western Union defended the deal. So did a few old whalers and fishermen. But the purchase was generally denounced. In the end, the Senate approved the treaty, but with only one vote more than the required two thirds. When the House was asked to appropriate the purchase money, there was an angry revolt. Thus, Dennis McCarthy, a New

An early prospector

York Republican, told the House that "every foot of the soil of Alaska is frozen from five to six feet in depth." Seward finally got the appropriation passed, but he had to launch a nation-wide publicity campaign in friendly newspapers. There were ugly rumors, backed by some evidence but never definitively proved, that influential members of Congress were bribed. Stoeckl told his government that most of the $200,000 added by Seward to the purchase price was used for "secret expenses." He also asked to be transferred to another post so he could "breathe an atmosphere purer than that of Washington."

So on October 18, 1867, the American flag went up that flagpole in Sitka. The greatest significance of more than a hundred years of Russian exploration and colonization in Alaska turned out to be its ending in American hands. If England had discovered Alaska, it would have remained part of Canada. But its control by a weaker, more distant power turned out to be fortunate for the United States in the long run.

For a little while the purchase stirred new hope in Sitka. There was an influx of hundreds of Americans, businessmen, frontiersmen, squatters, speculators—the kind of people, good and bad, who built up the West. But Washington had already forgotten about Alaska. There was no provision for acquiring land, filing claims, setting up local governments, no plans for developing the new territory, no criminal or civil code. There wasn't even military law. General Jefferson C. Davis, who had commanded the American troops at the flag-raising, remained with a few hundred soldiers. But he had no authority except to defend Alaska from foreign attack and hostile Indians.

It was expected that the soldiers would soon be replaced by a civil government. But Congress, disgusted with its new empire, failed to act. The soldiers stayed—and soon became a source of lawlessness. They were drunk and disorderly, debauched the Indian women, promoted distillation of a deadly "hoochenoo" of molasses and sugar to replace the old Indian home brew, and alienated the natives who had hoped that the exchange of masters would improve their conditions. The Russians, who were given an option of leaving or becoming United States citizens, sailed for home. So did most of the American settlers.

The soldiers left after ten years to fight the Nez Percé tribe in Idaho. Now the remaining settlers were terrified. They feared momentary attack from the Thlinget Indians. They appealed to the British for a warship to protect them, and a British ship from Vancouver Island was at Sitka for a while. Finally an American warship arrived, and for a time Navy rule of a sort replaced the Army. There was also a period when a Treasury customs collector was the highest United States official in Alaska.

Before Congress completely forgot about Alaska, it did remember to make Alaska a customs district. It also passed in 1870 "An act to prevent the extermination of the fur-bearing animals in Alaska." The effect was the exact opposite of that stated. This was a law authorizing the government to turn over exclusive seal-hunting rights on the Pribilof Islands to a group of businessmen residing mainly in San Francisco. The Alaska Commercial Company replaced the Russian-American Company and took over all its property.

After the new company was given a monopoly, no further legis-

A pioneer church in Juneau, photographed in 1885,
used also by the miners as a meeting hall

lation of any kind on Alaska was passed for many years. It was
charged that the oversight was not completely accidental. The
Alaska Commercial Company was not anxious to open up Alaska.
This would have invited competition with its sealing and with
its flourishing fur-hunting in the Yukon. Alaska had been a company possession under the Russians, and it virtually reverted to
that status under the United States.

Senator Ernest Gruening, governor of Alaska from 1939 to
1953, has written this bitter comment on early United States rule:
"During that period in Alaska no hopeful settler could acquire a
title to land; no pioneer could clear a bit of the forested wilderness
and count on the fruits of his toil, or build a log cabin with the
assurance that it was his; no prospector could stake a mining
claim with security for his enterprise; property could not be deeded
or transferred; no will was valid; marriage could not be celebrated;
no injured party could secure redress for grievances except through
his own acts; crime could not be punished."

YUKON ORDER OF PIONEERS 40 MILE 1895

GORDON BEETLES. PETE M°DONALD. BARNEY HILL. FRANK BUTEAU. GEO.MATLOCK. AL.MAYO. JOHN.NELSON. BILLY.LOYD. J. O'DONELL. L.La FLEM-
JAS.KENEDY. M.SCALES. PETE.NELSON.
H. HAMILTON HART. BILL.M°PHEE.   N. PICOTTE   L.N.M°QUESTION   FRANK BOKER.   HARRY RIVERS   JO.NAVARRO.

How long this state of affairs might have continued is anybody's guess. But there had long been rumors of gold in Alaska. Hardy prospectors kept looking. In 1880 Joseph Juneau and Richard Harris found gold in a creek in southeast Alaska. Other miners rushed in, made new discoveries in the area, founded a town which eventually became known as Juneau.

The discovery of gold helped prod a forgetful Congress. In 1884 Congress finally got around to passing an organic law for Alaska. Alaska was set up as a district with a civil governor and a semblance of civil law. A judicial district was created with a judge and other law-enforcement authorities. There was still no elected government of any kind. Congress levied no taxes. There was no land law governing settlement and property. But the mining laws of the United States were applied to Alaska. It was now possible for prospectors to file legal claims.

Two big mines developed at Juneau out of scattered claims, the Treadwell and the Alaska-Juneau mines, both owned largely

A shipyard where the prospectors of 1898 built their own boats
to float down the lakes to Dawson

by absentee, including British, capital. Juneau was chiefly hard-rock mining country. It needed heavy equipment to take the gold out and mill it. The prospectors continued to look in the Yukon area.

George Washington Carmack, a prospector who had gone native and married an Indian girl, was drawn to the Yukon after the strike in Juneau. Together with two of his wife's brothers, he found gold in late July 1896 on Rabbit Creek, later renamed Bonanza Creek, in Canadian Yukon Territory. Miners started pouring in from the whole surrounding area. By midsummer 1897 the discovery had made national headlines. Robert W. Service has described the impact:

> Gold! We leapt from our benches. Gold! We
> sprang from our stools . . .

Prospectors carting their supplies and worldly goods
over the trail in 1898

> Men from the sands of the Sunland; men from the
>   woods of the West;
> Men from the Farm and cities; into the North-
>   land we pressed.
> Graybeards and striplings and women, good men
>   and bad men and bold.
> Leaving our homes and our loved ones, crying
>   exultantly—"Gold!"

There were two major routes into the Yukon. One was to come
up the inside passage by ship and then by foot up steep mountain
passes, finally by boat on lakes and swift rivers much the rest of
the way. Many were killed by avalanches, blizzards, starvation.
Nevertheless thousands came in search of gold. In 1900 the build-

(Top) Rocking for gold on the Nome beach, and
(bottom) an old prospector's winter hut

Steadman Avenue, Nome, in July 1900

ing of the White Horse and Yukon Railroad (it was called "Wait patiently and you'll ride" by its eager customers) eased the trip somewhat. The other way, which took longer at a time when everyone was in a hurry, was to go by ship to St. Michael on the Bering Sea and then by river boat on the Yukon across the breadth of Alaska. How many came will never be known. But Canadian Mounted Police reported that by the end of 1898 some 30,000 persons had passed their registration post. Some of them found gold; most did not.

In 1898 there was another big gold strike, this time at Anvil Creek, near Nome, by a group of Swedes and Laplanders who had come as experts on the reindeer brought in to save the Eskimos from starvation. New discoveries were made on the beaches at Nome, and thousands of would-be prospectors came pouring off every boat from Seattle. Every foot of beach was filled with tents.

Two Fairbanks miners weighing in the cleanup of their placer mine

Overnight Nome became a bulging, roaring frontier city. At the height of the stampede, a dispute broke out over some of the claims. Enter at this point a movie villain from the badlands of North Dakota. Alexander McKenzie, a big-time politico with influence in the White House, was an owner of a mining company which bought up the interests of a number of claim-jumpers.

McKenzie arrived in Nome, bringing in tow Judge Arthur H. Noyes who had been sent in to hear the mine disputes. Noyes promptly appointed McKenzie, an interested party, receiver of the disputed claims. Virtual civil war broke out. In the end right triumphed. Noyes was found in contempt of the appeals court in San Francisco. McKenzie and some of his associates were jailed. The original claimants won out—but not before the Alaska miners were badly shaken in their already wavering faith in the kind of justice they could get from the federal government. The whole incident is described in literary technicolor in *The Spoilers* by Rex Beach.

Felix Pedro, an Italian miner, made the next big strike in the Tanana Valley in July 1902. He found the placer mines in the

Soapy Smith (his official name was Jefferson Randolph Smith) shown
standing at the bar (forefront) in one of his enterprises in Skagway

neighborhood of what is now Fairbanks. Within a few months
Fairbanks was a flourishing little town with a newspaper of its
own. The first issue ran this notice:

THE FAIRBANKS MINER

Published occasionally at Fairbanks, Alaska, by a stampeder who is
waiting for the snow to melt and the ice to go out of the rivers. The
paper will be mailed as soon as the Postmaster General establishes
the first Post Office in the Tanana Valley, to our living subscribers at
the regular subscription price of an ounce. Single copies $5.00 chee-
chaco money. No more advertisements wanted;—public notices refused—rate too low. If you don't like our style fly your kite and produce your 30-30.

There was a zest and a broad humor here typical of the veterans of the Alaska gold rush. The sourdoughs managed to keep

Pioneers' Home in Sitka

laughing despite hardships and disasters. Few struck it rich, and most of those who did lost it one way or another. Some were defrauded and victimized. Only a handful were able to exploit the discoveries they did make.

You can meet some of the survivors today at the Pioneers' Home in Sitka, gnarled old men who never made it or were wiped out at cards or by fire or by trickery. This is one of the few public institutions for the aged where rules are at a minimum, where inmates are called guests and are treated as such. They can leave at any time and return at will. This is partly because these independent oldsters would have it no other way, partly because of the respect with which Alaska treats its pioneers.

The sourdoughs have no doubt been romanticized by London and Beach and Service. But they had to be a tough and rugged breed to endure the hardships of the overland trails and to keep plugging away year after year. They were not for the most part lawless or violent men, and they had a loyal fellowship of their own. A character in *The Spoilers* puts it this way: "There weren't any crimes in this country till the tenderfeet arrived. We didn't know what a thief was. If you came to a cabin you walked in without knocking. The owner filled up the coffee-pot and sliced into the bacon; then when he'd started your meal, he shook hands, and asked your name . . . If there was no one at home, you took what you needed." There were desperados, of course, like that colorful rogue, Soapy Smith, who commanded a band of crooks and highwaymen that controlled the trails into the Klondike and collected a rich booty from the travelers. But Beach would have dismissed them as tenderfeet or at any rate not real sourdoughs.

The miners maintained a rough frontier democracy, providing in many cases the only law there was in the interior. They were in the forefront of Alaska's many fights for self-government, and they were bitter at those who, they felt, robbed Alaska of its birthright—at absentee owners and an absentee government in Washington.

The gold rush swelled Alaska's population. By 1900 it was 63,-592, half of it white, and it continued to rise for several years. But the torrent of new settlers gradually subsided. A few concessions were won as a result of all the excitement. In 1912 Alaskans were finally granted a territorial form of government in the Organic Act of Alaska. But Washington did little to develop the area or to open the land up for settlement. Homesteading laws were hemmed in with restrictions. The laws on placer mining tended to favor bigger companies rather than the prospectors on the creeks and rivers.

Step by step a small group of powerful interests entrenched themselves in Alaska. For a time the dominant group was the Alaska Syndicate formed by J. P. Morgan & Company and the Guggenheim mining interests. This combine acquired the Bonanza copper mine, built a railroad to its mining properties, took over controlling interest in the Alaska Steamship Company, and bought a dozen canneries. Soon Alaska slipped back into oblivion. There were big profits for a time from its copper and gold as well

as a steady yield from salmon. But its economy as a whole stag-
nated, and its population dropped. There were fewer people in
Alaska in 1930 than in 1900. Its resources were not being developed, its potential not being realized.

Sam Dunham, an old sourdough poet, summed up the senti-
ments of Alaskans, not only at the time but for many years to
come, when he wrote in 1901:

> Sitting on my greatest glacier,
>   with my feet in Bering Sea,
> I am thinking cold and lonely,
>   of the way you've treated me.
> Three and thirty years of silence!
> Through ten thousand sleeping nights
> I've been praying for your coming,
>   for the dawn of civil rights.
>
> When you took me, young and trusting,
>   from the growling Russian Bear,
> Loud you swore before the Nation
>   I should have the Eagle's care.
> Never yet has wing of Eagle
>   cast a shadow on my peaks,
> But I've watched the flight of buzzards
>   and I've felt their busy beaks.

3: A World Crossroads

On Wednesday, September 17, 1958, at 11:05 A.M., a sleek DC7C arrived at the Fairbanks International Airport from Tokyo. The plane was on a trial run for Royal Dutch Airlines, which shortly afterwards inaugurated a transpolar route between Europe and Asia with an operational stop in Alaska. This was a pioneering flight for KLM, but two other European airlines had started similar routes earlier, and several others were actively considering the new short cut between Europe and Asia.

With the coming of the air age, Alaska ended its long sojourn in the international twilight, a vast backwater far removed from all centers of world population. The big peninsula jutting out into the North Pacific has now become the bridge to Asia of which Seward dreamed when he purchased Alaska. It has become the short cut to the East sought by generations of hardy mariners.

Twenty years before the big airliners started flying over Alaska, James Wickersham, a remarkable Alaska pioneer widely regarded as the father of statehood, wrote with almost prophetic vision:

Draw a line from New York to Fairbanks, and from Fairbanks to Tokyo, Shanghai and Manila, over the surface of your library globe; it is the shortest distance between America and those Asiatic capitals. When inter-continental aviation is perfected, the safest and shortest flying line will naturally follow this great circle.

41

The air age comes to Alaska

Wickersham was mistaken only in a minor detail. Because its airport has superior facilities, Anchorage has become the stopping-off point in Alaska for the major airlines, Fairbanks for the time being the alternate stop. But certainly Alaska's importance on international air routes is now generally recognized. Anchorage, for example, ranks fourth nationally in total air traffic of the United States. Alaska is also recognized as an area of immense strategic importance, its geographic locale central in both war and peace.

By the time World War II was well under way, Washington had finally rediscovered the Territory. It had grasped both the meaning of its strategic location and the potential of its vast natural riches. But it took a war to do it, and in a real sense it was the Japanese who rediscovered Alaska for us.

The United States was totally unprepared for war in Alaska. It paid, and paid dearly, for almost three quarters of a century of

The old Chilkoot Barracks—only U. S. defense outpost
in Alaska when World War II started

neglect. When World War II started in 1939, there was one military post, Chilkoot Barracks, in all Alaska. It was stuck off in a
corner of southeast Alaska, and had 250 officers and men to guard
some 586,000 square miles. The soldiers were armed with Spring-
field rifles. There was not even an anti-aircraft gun at the barracks.

A few dissenting voices had protested this state of affairs. Briga-
dier General William (Billy) Mitchell had been arguing for years
for Alaska air bases. In 1935, shortly before his death, he told a
House Military Affairs Committee hearing: "Japan is our dangerous enemy in the Pacific. They won't attack Panama. They
will come right here to Alaska. Alaska is the most central place
in the world for aircraft." Anthony J. Dimond, Alaska's delegate
to Congress, kept banging away on the same theme. "Defend the
United States by defending Alaska," he said on the House floor as
early as 1934.

It wasn't until 1939 that appropriations were made for an Army
cold-weather testing station for airplanes near Fairbanks and for

(Top) U. S. soldiers in Alaska, and (bottom) newcomers

naval air stations at Sitka and Kodiak. As late as March 1940 the House Appropriations Committee eliminated a $13,000,000 item for an Army air base at Anchorage. The committee reversed itself after the Nazis started marching through Europe that spring. In 1941 the Navy didn't even have charts for some of the smaller Aleutian Islands.

The Army finally began early in 1942 to take serious steps to defend Alaska. Under cover of secrecy, supplies were rushed to a nonexistent company, Blair and Caxton, with mythical fish canneries on the Alaska Peninsula and the Aleutians. Work was begun at bases on Cold Bay and Unimak. The Navy had also taken steps to build a base at Dutch Harbor in the Aleutians as well as at Sitka and Kodiak. But when the Japanese attacked Pearl Harbor, not a single air or naval base in Alaska had been completed.

The Japanese had evidently been preparing to strike at Alaska for a long time. Japanese fishing vessels had been going up and down the Aleutians for years, had even put in at Bristol Bay on the Alaska Peninsula. There were undoubtedly bona-fide fishing boats among them. But many of the vessels had Japanese Navy officers aboard. While U.S. meteorological stations in Alaska were decidedly inadequate, Japanese weather stations had made a careful study of the uncertain and stormy weather in the Aleutians.

When the Japanese bombed our base at Dutch Harbor on June 3, 1942, it was part of a major two-pronged attack. Far to the south, the main Japanese naval force made for Midway Island. Navy patrol planes gave the alarm in time, and the Navy decisively defeated the Japanese at the battle of Midway. If Midway had been taken, the Japanese would have had northern and southern bases for striking at the continental United States.

They made some initial gains in the Aleutians. When the first wave of Japanese fighters flew over Dutch Harbor, there was no alarm—and there were no American fighter planes to stop them. The Zeros withdrew to their carrier bases. Heavy bombers came the next day, but the Navy rallied and offered stiff resistance. So the Japanese swung farther south in the Aleutians and seized Attu and Kiska Islands.

They meant to hold the islands, too. They built elaborate underground runways and trenches, and sent in reinforcements. When United States troops landed on Attu on May 11, 1943, the Japanese fought back from foxholes and machine gun nests in the mountains. It took two months and more than 1,500 casualties before the island was taken. The Japanese evacuated Kiska without a battle. But the Aleutian campaign as a whole cost some 2,500 American lives.

The Japanese fought stubbornly for a base from which to at-

Lookouts on U. S. submarine returning from war patrol

tack our own west coast and from which they hoped to cut off a growing supply line between the United States and the Soviet Union. Alaska became an important junction in the delivery of military planes to Russia. Readying planes for the Russians was one of the major jobs of Ladd Air Force Base near Fairbanks. The first group of Russian pilots arrived in September 1942 and

Members of the 1st Eskimo Scout Battalion of the Alaska
National Guard receiving markmanship training
at Fort Richardson

took off with 12 A-20's for the Soviet Union; and this military traffic picked up steadily. Alaska's importance as an air crossroads was amply demonstrated.

World War II put Alaska on the map in more ways than one. Thousands of young men discovered Alaska for the first time. It is estimated that 300,000 members of the Armed Forces were stationed there. Many liked what they saw and returned when the war was over. You run into them all over Alaska, men in their late thirties or early forties who now hold responsible positions in industry, government, and air transportation. Restless after the war, they found in Alaska their land of opportunity.

The war drew the native population into the mainstream of

Alaskan life. The Alaska National Guard enlisted hundreds of Eskimos and Aleuts in scout battalions. They served valiantly in the Aleutians. In the armed forces, Alaska's natives received opportunities to acquire technical training they badly needed if they were to be integrated into modern life. The Eskimos showed themselves particularly adaptable in learning mechanical skills. Many, emerging from the war as pilots and mechanics, got jobs either with local airlines or with the military services.

The war revived the civilian economy with vast injections of military spending. Alaska had not been as hard hit as the rest of the United States during the depression. Gold mining had even taken something of a spurt. Many unemployed workers and some farmers had come to Alaska in search of opportunity. But it was the war that resulted in a big boom for Alaska. Costly installations had to be built, bases, harbors, air fields, weather stations, tent cities and then wooden housing for construction workers, roads, oil pipelines. Many of the wartime facilities were of direct importance to the civilian economy and were used after the war.

One of the most important projects resulting from World War II was the Alaska Highway, originally called the Alcan, linking the United States and Alaska through Canada. This had been a dream for decades. There was support for the idea both in Alaska and in the Canadian Yukon. A favorable report was made by an international commission in 1930. There were more reports, more commissions. Pearl Harbor put an end to the interminable delays. On Feb. 11, 1942, President Roosevelt assented to the plan. The Canadian government promptly approved, and work started in a few weeks.

It was an immense job. The Army moved in seven engineering battalions, four white, three Negro. There were 30,000 civilian laborers under 54 different contractors. The men worked ten-hour shifts, seven days a week. "This is no picnic," said a sign put up by one contractor in his hiring hall. "Working and living conditions on this job are as difficult as those encountered on any construction job ever done in the United States or foreign territory." An almost bottomless morass of muskeg, decayed vegetation, and water had to be attacked in northern British Columbia. The weather

Fort Richardson near Anchorage

was often too hot or too cold. Floods washed out the work. Layers of ice would block the road in winter. But by the spring of 1944 the last bridges were put in place.

Alaska at last had a highway connecting it with the United States by land. Branch roads had to be built, linking Fairbanks, Anchorage, Seward, and other important cities. The roads weren't perfect, but they were better than old wagon trails or no access at all. Alaska was emerging from its isolation.

The cities started growing rapidly during the war. New housing had to be constructed for the swelling military and civilian population. Federal matching funds helped build community facilities such as water and sewage plants. School buildings were constructed. The territorial legislature, under the leadership of then Governor Ernest Gruening, acted quickly to make possible the use of wartime facilities for civilian purposes. At the end of the war the legislature appropriated funds to combat the growing menace of tuberculosis among the native population. Agencies were set up to build Alaska's economy and to promote private and pub-

White Alice stations link military installations and also provide
communications for Alaska's scattered civilian communities

lic housing. Alaska provided veterans with bonuses—and loans up
to $10,000 to enable them to acquire homes, farms, businesses.

Whether this growth could have been sustained without substantial and continuing injections of federal funds for military purposes is a matter for conjecture. In any case, United States relations with Russia took a nose-dive in the late '40s and reached an
all-time low during the Korean War. Alaska's strategic position
and its proximity to Russia gave it top priority in the huge rearma-
ment program started under President Harry Truman. World War II
military installations were reactivated and expanded. New ones
were built. Alaska became a major military center for the United
States.

In the most remote Arctic villages today you will see radar
towers—outposts of the Dew Line, the distant early warning network, which will give the United States substantial advance notice

U. S. military hospital at Elmendorf Field near Anchorage

of any enemy attack. Peeking out from behind hills you will see in Nome and elsewhere great curved sheets supported by pylon-like towers. These are antennas of the White Alice communications system. There are also Nike installations near most of Alaska's larger population centers.

Fort Richardson and Elmendorf Field near Anchorage are two of the largest of Alaska's military installations. Here are headquarters for the Alaskan Command, co-ordinating all United States forces in Alaska, the Alaskan Air Command and the Army. Nearby, the Army maintains its own port at Whittier, with a $6,-000,000 multi-purpose building which provides facilities for 3,000 officers and men. Navy headquarters are at Kodiak, with the job of protecting Alaska's harbors and waters and keeping the Dew Line supplied.

Alaska has become a major center for experimentation in Arctic fighting. At Fort Greely, about 100 miles from Fairbanks, are the Army's Cold Weather and Mountain School, the Arctic Test Board, and the Chemical Corps Test Team. This is a neat and modern military installation. But the lawns are a bit ragged. A

Composite building at the Army port of Whittier—a bachelor city under one roof—containing housing, recreation centers, lounges, theaters, commissary, bank, hospital, PX, and hobby shops

herd of buffalo roaming the range in the area seems to prefer the Fort Greely grass. Wives of officers and men at Greely have complained at seeing the heads of big bison peeking into their bedroom windows.

Ladd Air Force Base near Fairbanks is the center for squadrons of fighter-interceptor jet planes. Here also is the Arctic Aeromedical Laboratory which has done extensive research on drugs to render persons more resistant to cold. Specialists at the laboratory have studied susceptibility to frost-bite and effectiveness of medical equipment under Arctic conditions. At Eielson Air Force Base, also near Fairbanks, are stationed the big bombers of the Strategic Air Command.

The impact of developing this huge military network in Alaska is enormous. Thousands of construction workers, both local labor-

Soldiers take off from Ladd Air Base for a patrol of
remote areas in far north

ers and craftsmen brought in from the states, were required for
the more than $800,000,000 spent for construction in the decade
following the end of World War II. Anchorage and Fairbanks, the
major centers of military installations, both boomed. While stateside contractors did most of the work, a good-sized construction
industry also developed in Alaska itself. Construction has now
perceptibly slowed down. Most of the major projects have been
completed. But some new military installations have been projected
—including a $300,000,000 anti-missile center at Clear in the
north.

Alaska's continuing growth in population from 1950 to the present has been due in large part to the defense programs. There have
been about 50,000 military personnel stationed in Alaska for the
last few years. In addition, there have been thousands of depend-
ents of servicemen and officers as well as thousands of civilian
personnel on military payrolls. A great deal of new housing
had to be constructed. Service trades and small industry developed.

But a war economy has its disadvantages. Anchorage, for exam-

Ultramodern apartment building for Army families at
the military port of Whittier

ple, spurted forward during the big defense build-up of the early
1950's, then was hard hit by sharp cut-backs in the number of
military personnel and by the completion of major construction
projects. Personnel on military payrolls in the Anchorage area
dropped from 32,000 in 1955 to 19,000 in 1958. Many of those
dropped from the payrolls or shifted elsewhere were living off-base.
An acute housing shortage suddenly became a substantial surplus
of new and expensive apartments. Jobs which had gone begging
became scarce, and there was substantial unemployment.

Anchorage has gradually pulled out of its slump. Developing
trades and industries have absorbed some of the unemployed. Anchorage businessmen still expect the military establishment to play
a key role in their area's economy. But they are also looking for
new industries and new sources of employment. An advisory com-

mittee of business and civic leaders reported with some pride in mid-1958: "The basic economy of the community is no longer so starkly dependent upon the military establishments as in the past." Alaska obviously needs a healthy peacetime economy if it is to survive sudden or drastic changes in military planning.

Alaska is in a paradoxical position. On the one hand, its growth and prosperity have been promoted by war and its aftermath. On the other hand, its future economic welfare depends on peace. The many indirect benefits accruing from the last war would be swept away in a new war. Heightened wartime interest in Alaska brought new population, an increased number of tourists, new interest by American and foreign business interests. Many new possibilities developed. But these will be realized only if there is some relaxation of international tensions, or at least no worsening of the present situation.

Oil and metal mining industries, for example, require heavy capital investments. These are hardly likely to materialize if investors have serious reason to believe that Alaska will become an international trouble spot. The same is true of Alaska's prospects for increased population and for building up tourism. Alaska needs at least a semblance of peace to develop its position on international air routes.

Three airlines have picked Anchorage for operational flight stops on flights between Europe and Asia. The Scandinavian Air System pioneered the route in 1957, and KLM and Air France subsequently instituted similar flights. Japan Airlines and the German Lufthansa have also been actively considering the new transpolar short cut via Alaska. The economic importance of these flights is considerable. Anchorage businessmen estimate that each airline with stop-over facilities spends about $1,000,000 a year in the area. This amount will, of course, be increased substantially if foreign airlines win approval for applications to pick up and leave passengers at Anchorage. Such a development would open up Alaska to European tourists.

The interest of Japan Airlines in an air route via Anchorage is symptomatic. The Japanese, who long ago discovered the importance of Alaska and tried to occupy it in wartime as a military

The S. S. Olympia Maru stopping at Sitka

base, are also keenly aware of its peacetime potential. Alaska is close enough to Japan to become one of its principal sources of raw materials. Japanese businessmen have been looking into the possibilities of developing Alaskan oil and coking coal for import. In fact, one of the largest new industrial developments in the forty-ninth state is due to Japanese enterprise.

Don't be surprised, if you visit Sitka, to see a sleek little Japanese auto, the Toyopet Crown Deluxe. It belongs to a Japanese engineer at the $55,000,000 pulp mill under construction there. The mill is being financed largely by Japanese capitalists anxious to take advantage of southeast Alaska's luxuriant forests to provide pulp for their rayon and synthetics industries. Japanese merchant ships have been laying in at Sitka, Wrangell and Ketchikan as an outgrowth of their interest in Alaska lumber and pulp.

The first visit of a Japanese ship, M.S. *Olympia Maru,* to Sitka in March 1958 was watched a bit nervously both by Japanese officials and by local residents. Wartime memories are still fresh in Alaska. But the visit passed off smoothly enough. There was an official welcome to the guests, and Japanese dolls were presented to the Pioneers' Home, schools, hospitals, and other institutions.

Two worlds meet in this aerial view of Big Diomede and Little Diomede
Islands—to the left is American territory, to the right Russian

Alaskans have mixed feelings about the larger role Japanese
capital is beginning to play in their economy. There is still some
hostility to Japan, and there is considerable bitterness by fishermen over the continued fishing by Japanese vessels off Alaskan
waters. A few shooting forays between Japanese and American
fishermen have been reported. But most Alaskans believe that
Japan's need for their raw materials will be beneficial. They also
hope that Japanese investment will prod American businessmen.
As one official in Juneau puts it, "If Japanese investors have faith
in the future of Alaska, perhaps American business leaders will
develop similar faith."

Of course, feelings of Alaska about Russia are even more
sharply mixed. There is a combination of apprehension, curiosity,
and cautious hope for better relations in the future. On the one
hand, Alaskans are used to regarding Russia, only fifty miles
away across the Bering Strait, as the enemy against whom our
vast military installations have been constructed. On the other
hand, the proximity is a source of interest. So is the Russian period
in Alaska's history. Hundreds of Alaskans are studying Russian.
An agricultural specialist tells you that Russia's successes in growing crops in Siberia are a challenge to Alaska. A Fairbanks businessman says, "I have no use for Russia, but they are certainly

managing to build a civilization in the North. We can learn from them."

The interest increases the farther west you go, the closer you get to Russia. J. G. Manning, executive manager of the Miners and Merchants Bank of Nome, is asked what prospects he sees for economic growth in what was once a roaring gold rush town but is now a rather stagnant backwater. He mentions a number of possibilities: the impact of a projected road to connect Nome with the interior, untapped mineral resources, a growth in tourist trade. Then he looks out across the Bering Sea from his office, the waves breaking on the sea wall. He says, "Of course, the State Department will have to make the decisions." But international air travel to Moscow would put Nome on the map. One airline has already applied for a regular commercial flight. Nome would be a logical port of entry.

Mrs. Emily Boucher, publisher of the *Nome Nugget,* also stresses the possibility of travel and trade with Russia as a boost for the economy of western Alaska. She even mentions the old dream of a bridge or a tunnel across the Bering Strait to Siberia.

Early in the century Edward H. Harriman, the railroad magnate, talked of building a railroad from the United States across the breadth of Alaska and then to the Bering Strait where it would connect with a Russian railroad. In recent years a road connection rather than a railroad has appeared more intriguing. Russians have from time to time suggested the possibility of a bridge across the strait. American engineers have speculated about construction of a tunnel. If this hope is ever realized, auto travel virtually around the world would then become feasible. Obviously the time for such a project is not yet. But if it is ever realized, Alaska would truly become a world crossroads, a link between America, Asia, and Europe.

4: The First Alaskans

Roy Peratrovich looks like the typical businessman anywhere: dark suit, striped tie, glasses. His skin is perhaps a bit darker, his cheekbones maybe a little higher. Peratrovich happens to be Indian, his name an inheritance from some long-forgotten Russian ancestor. He is a loan examiner for the Alaska Native Service in Juneau. His job is to pass on government loans to Indian small business for fishing boats, general stores, and canneries owned co-operatively by a whole village.

This is the kind of success story Alaskans like to tell you about. Peratrovich came out of the little southeast Alaskan fishing village of Klawock. He went to a village Indian school, was an exceptional student, went to Bellingham Normal College in Washington state on a scholarship, then went to the University of Denver at night, studying finance during the day at a bank. He worked hard, assisted by fellowships from the John Hay Whitney Foundation and the United Nations. Now he is a successful and respected citizen. His brother Frank, a territorial senator for a number of years, is now a state senator.

White Alaskans often point with pride to the achievements and capabilities of the native population. There is considerable to point to. The pilot of your plane flying north to the Arctic may well turn out to be an Eskimo, natty in his uniform, tall and well built, dis-

Eskimo soldiers, members of Alaska National Guard Scout Battalion,
marking targets during firing practice

tinguishable from his passengers only by the somewhat Asian bone
structure of his face. There are a few native officials of airlines
and other companies. There are Eskimo and Aleut technicians on
the Dew Line and the White Alice communications system. There
are skilled winchmen on the big gold dredges in Nome.

You find substantial evidence of good will toward the aspirations of the native peoples. A Chamber of Commerce official in
Anchorage may floor the visitor by volunteering the information
that the cranium of the Eskimo is the largest known to man. Or a
businessman in Fairbanks may single out the technical aptitude of
Alaska's natives. The good will has been made tangible by the
election of about half a dozen Indians and Eskimos in recent years

A typical Alaska vista—restored totem poles at Klawock
guarding a salmon cannery

to the Alaska legislature. White votes helped to elect them to office.

Certainly Eskimos and Indians do not face the encrusted segregation prevalent in the American South or the pervasive hostility to their desires for advancement and equality. In the old days, and even as recently as World War II, "No natives served here" signs were a familiar sight in Juneau and other cities. These were outlawed by the legislature in 1945. Segregation in the school system has also been eliminated. Discrimination in employment was banned by the legislature in 1955. "There is no racial problem in Alaska," says Senator Ernest Gruening.

This is part of the story, and an important part. "But you don't

Eskimo homes in the village of Kotzebue

always hear the whole story," says Peratrovich. "There is a good secondary school for native children at Mt. Edgecumbe. But it is hopelessly overcrowded. It doesn't have enough funds or facilities. Hundreds of children from the villages can't get in." He cites statistics which show that native children in Alaska get 5½ years schooling on the average, about half the average for white children.

"There aren't enough opportunities for jobs," Peratrovich continues. "Indians and Eskimos can't sustain themselves any more by hunting, fishing and picking berries. Our people in southeast Alaska are too dependent on the fishing industry, and fishing has been very poor the last few years. There aren't enough job opportunities to go around. When there are jobs, the natives are often the last hired. There are too few jobs for them in the government, except in the Native Service."

One of Peratrovich's sons, a graduate of the University of Washington, is now an assistant city engineer in Seattle. "I saw to it that

Two little Alaskans enjoy a sunny day at the beach

he didn't have to struggle the way we had to," Peratrovich says.

"Why doesn't he work in Alaska?"

"Well, it would be hard for him to get a job of the same stature here."

Peratrovich is the head of the Alaska Native Brotherhood, an organization of Indians described by some as a small-scale National Association for the Advancement of Colored People. Its battles in former years were largely for civil rights and against discrimination. Now it seeks to assure education and opportunity for the Indian.

Housing is still a major problem of Alaska's natives, especially in the villages. But in the cities, too, their homes are usually inadequate and in the poor sections of town. Their economy in the native villages is precarious, their position in the cities still not solidified. Alaska's native population is in transition between the old and the

Eskimo girl in summer parka with sled dog

new. They can no longer make a living in the old way. On the other hand, they have not yet been fully integrated into the new. In a larger sense, their problem is tied to the future of Alaska. As Alaska grows and develops, their opportunities will increase.

There is no doubt that Alaska's natives have come a long way in a relatively short time. While the white man has been in Alaska on

Indian children at a Greek Orthodox Church ceremony in Sitka

and off for some two hundred years, the native usually encountered the less savory aspects of Western civilization. It is only in the relatively recent past that some of the benefits have also been made available. In the last few decades the United States has done much to redress the wrongs done to the native population. But there has been much to redress. The natives of Alaska suffered in their first contacts with white civilization as did aboriginal peoples almost everywhere.

The Aleuts lived peacefully enough on their islands and on the southern coast of the Bering Sea. They were sea hunters. They relied on the sea for food and clothing, sometimes making long voyages in their single- or double-hatched light skin boats after

Old burial ground in the Indian village of Elkutna with little houses
in which were put household goods and clothing for the departed
until their spirits left for the "happy hunting ground"

sea otters, seals, sea lions, and even whales. When the Russians
came, there were about 25,000 Aleuts. By the time the United
States took over, there were only about 4,000 left. The Russians
killed off many in their early years in Alaska and virtually en-
slaved most of the others to hunt for furs. The Aleuts were converted to the Greek Orthodox Church, and a few were educated in
mission schools. Most of them now are of mixed blood.

The southeast Indians had developed a high culture of their own.
The Thlingets were great traders, and they made the famed Chilkat
blanket from the wool of the mountain goat, using designs sym-
bolic of their various clans. They were skilled wood carvers, as
they showed in their totem poles, a relatively recent development,

Southeast Indians stage an almost extinct tribal ceremony

which served both as a coat of arms of the clan and a historical record. They were also fishermen and hunters, and perhaps a more warlike people. They certainly gave the Russians a great deal of trouble, but they were finally ravaged by conquest and disease. The culture of the Interior Indians, the Athabascans, was on a lower level. Their life was harder and more rugged. Their contact with the white man came somewhat later, but was even more fatal. They succumbed in large numbers to measles and smallpox.

The Aleuts' culture was related to that of the Eskimos. Indeed, all the native peoples of Alaska are remotely related. They came from Asia thousands of years ago; whether by land or water or ice no one is sure, although many experts believe that Asia and

Eskimo dance—a survival of an old culture

America were once connected by land across the Bering Strait. The great anthropologist, Aleš Hrdlička, held firmly to this view. The Eskimos were probably early arrivals. Discoveries on the Point Hope Peninsula—far in the north—of stone, jade and bone hunting implements dating back at least two thousand years point to an old and developed civilization. The Eskimos, a hardy and ingenious people, overcame and survived the rigors of the Arctic. In frail craft of driftwood covered with skins they hunted the whale and the walrus.

The Eskimos largely escaped the Russians. But the Yankee whalers who arrived in Arctic waters around 1850 introduced them to such blessings of civilization as whiskey, firearms, the harpoon gun, prostitution, and slavery. The Western Union expedition in the 1860's brought syphilis and later came T.B., to which the Eskimos were particularly susceptible.

To most of the natives, American rule did not seem much of an improvement at first. The soldiers sold them whiskey and the ingredients for a more powerful "hoochenoo," and debauched their women. There were frequent clashes between the Indians and soldiers during the early period of American rule.

One scourge brought by the white man which still lingers is T.B. The natives had no immunity to T.B., and thousands of them died from it. Bad housing conditions and poor sanitation have perpetuated the disease. As recently as 1954, the known case rate among the native peoples was 245.6 for every 10,000 of the population. This was almost five times as high as among Indians in the United States—and about forty times as high as the T.B. rate among the general United States population. Considerable progress has been made in recent years in checking T.B. among the natives. In 1956, fifty native deaths from T.B. were reported. This was still high, but the death rate had dropped to less than a quarter of what it had been in 1950. Several native hospitals cope with the problem. These are inadequate, however, and beds in community hospitals in Alaska and in Washington state are also used for the native T.B. patients.

But in all the disasters that befell Alaska's natives, they were more fortunate than the American Indians in one important respect. They were not pushed off the land. Alaska was not populated by white men to the same degree, and the natives were not crowded onto the least promising land in reservations. Thus they had a base for survival when conditions began to improve.

They were also more fortunate in some of the missionaries who came to them from the United States. In Sheldon Jackson, a Presbyterian missionary, they found a real champion. Jackson and his associates were often blind to, or intolerant of, the native culture. For example, he was shocked by the community houses in which the Thlinget and other native peoples lived. He said that in such houses "where fifty or sixty men, women and children lived huddled together, no decency, no modesty, no morality, and no sani-

Abraham Lincoln totem made by Indians during the early period
of American rule to remind the United States of the pledges
of the Great Emancipator

tation are possible." The natives' old customs and religion were quickly disposed of. Their totem poles, scorned as pagan relics, were permitted to fall into disrepair. Nevertheless Jackson was sincerely interested in improving their lot; he did fight to establish schools for natives and to get appropriations for their welfare. When in 1877 he was appointed the government's general agent of education in Alaska, he was often accused by the whites of favoring the natives.

Jackson devoted himself to the material as well as the spiritual welfare of the native people. It was Jackson who intervened when the Eskimos verged on starvation in 1890. White whalers had killed off the Eskimos' principle source of life—the whale—and then proceeded to slaughter the walrus. The natives turned to caribou, which were also killed in large numbers. So Jackson brought in reindeer from Siberia and herders from Lapland to instruct the Eskimos in their use. These reindeer were for many years afterward a mainstay of the Eskimo economy.

Under Jackson's vigorous leadership, schools were built in Indian, Eskimo, and Aleut villages. Many of the children were taught crafts and skills. Today native children in the cities and the larger villages go to public schools with white children. But there are still of necessity native schools in remote, isolated villages. There is also the fine native high school at Mt. Edgecumbe near Sitka.

Every September there is a massive airlift to bring about 600 boys and girls from the small villages all over Alaska to this boarding school. Bush pilots—an extraordinarily daring and resourceful group on the Alaska scene—pick up the students from the most isolated communities, bringing them to central points such as Anchorage, Fairbanks, Nome. Then they are transported by major airlines first to southeast Alaska and finally to Sitka.

The youngsters at Mt. Edgecumbe look and act like typical teenagers anywhere. The girls wear skirts and sweaters and the inevitable bobby sox, the boys jeans and sport shirts. In good weather a basketball game may be in progress on the spacious school grounds, once used for a naval base. Or girls in middy blouses may be doing calisthenics. Many cannot be told from white children. There is, in fact, a surprising number of blond Nordic types at the school. The admission requirements are that the children be one quarter native; the differing racial mixtures result in considerable variety in appearance.

If there is any difference, it is that the percentage of serious students is probably higher than among white students of similar age. They have come a long way for their education and it means a good deal to them. *Taheeta,* their 1958 yearbook, presents the observations of the seniors next to their pictures in caps and gowns. A few offer flip comments, but very few. "As for my voice," says James Williams of Klawock, "I have lost it with hollering and singing of anthems." But Agnes Stepan of Alitak says: "If you want to travel fast, travel light. Take off all your jealousies, prejudices, selfishness and fears." The classes reflect this seriousness of purpose.

"What is the First Amendment to the Constitution?" asks social studies instructor Teresa Ripley.

"Freedom of speech and assembly," says an Eskimo boy up front.

An Indian boy in the rear raises his hand, adds earnestly, "But our freedoms are relative."

In another classroom, a young Negro typing instructor intones "KLM, KLM."

The boys and girls intently type out the letters on their new Underwood typewriters.

Many of the classes are vocational. Girls are instructed in nursing and home economics. Boys are taught a variety of crafts in a big converted hangar used by the Navy in World War II. Here they are given classes in Diesel engines, tractors, woodwork, aircraft frames and engines.

"Most of them will have to work with their hands," says Superintendent Robin R. Dean. "They might as well learn now. On the other hand, they get enough academic background to qualify for college and many continue their studies either at the University of Alaska or a number of colleges in Washington state."

The problem of overcrowding at Mt. Edgecumbe is serious. The dormitories are not big enough to provide adequate space for study, and this slows the pupils up. Moreover, the limited facilities

Mt. Edgecumbe School: (top left) students learning to work on
motors, (top right) a typing class, (bottom left) a class for
nurses, and (bottom right) a class of students confined
with T.B. at the Mt. Edgecumbe Island hospital

keep out hundreds of eligible boys and girls who apply for admission. "You should read some of their letters," says Dean. "They're heart-breaking."

But there is another problem, and it is often cited by critics of government expenditures for Mt. Edgecumbe and other services. "What happens when the graduates get back to the village?" they ask. "They sink back into old ways. It's a waste of money."

Of course, village life still has aspects of the primitive. Sanita-

Native boys and girls study painting

tion is often nonexistent, housing limited. Dog-sleds are still used in Eskimo villages and by the Indians in the Interior. The whale, walrus, and reindeer are still mainstays of the Eskimo economy. Many Indians still depend precariously on hunting and fishing and trapping. Eskimo women still skin and prepare the seal and oogruk as of old, preserving the blubber in a sealskin bag called a "seal poke." Women still sew furs for parkas and mukluks. Children still eat strips of dried salmon and reindeer meat or Eskimo ice cream, melted reindeer fat or seal oil beaten with fresh clean snow until it forms a creamy mass and mixed with blueberries.

But native spokesmen, as well as educators and others, argue in rebuttal that education is essential for better sanitation, improved

Eskimo woman making mukluks

health safeguards, gradual advance in the native way of life. They say that many young natives return to the villages from school as teachers and nurses. Others get the opportunity to pursue skilled crafts or professions in the cities. The government needs skilled technicians at remote defense installations. They point to new aspects of native life in which skills are needed. For example, both Eskimos and Indians now often use motors in their fishing boats.

Carrying a seal poke filled with the oil of three seals

Besides, many Alaskans see increased need for technical skills. They foresee the possibility of eventually modernizing and streamlining the native economy in the north. One Fairbanks businessman even talks of providing the Eskimos with helicopters to hunt whales.

Some Alaskans warn against indiscriminate modernization. They say there is sound sense in native foods which provide the fats necessary for protection against the elements. Too sudden Americanization can be harmful. They cite cases of Eskimo girls of 11 and 12 who are given candy by kind-hearted missionaries only to lose all their teeth. The point is made that not all of native life should be hastily discarded, that not all of the old values and arts and crafts should be rejected.

It is only in recent years that the artistic value of the totem pole has been appreciated. The Aleut villagers, once considered the

A group of totem poles in Southeast Alaska

greatest basket weavers in the world, have all but lost their ancient art. Preservation of the old arts is now considered of prime cultural value, and fine examples of native work are to be seen at the Territorial Museum in Juneau and at the Sheldon Jackson Museum in Sitka.

Handicrafts are now an important means of livelihood for many Eskimos and Indians. In recent years native craftsmen have been encouraged by the Alaska Native Service, as the Bureau of Indian Affairs is called in Alaska. With government help, a co-operative agency has been set up to market native art work. The Alaska Native Arts and Crafts Clearing House serves a twofold purpose.

(Top) Drawings of early Eskimo living; and, later (bottom),
a settlement with schools and churches for the Eskimos

It protects the craftsmen against cheap imitations, by wholesaling
and promoting miniature totem poles, Eskimo ceremonial masks,
Eskimo and Indian slippers, jewelry and walrus sculptures. It also
encourages the craftsmen to maintain and improve their standards,
and to reject inferior work.

One native artist who has won general recognition is George
Ahgupuk. Born in the little village of Shishmaref, he broke a leg
on a long sled trip when he was 19. At the Native Service hospital
he started making drawings on toilet paper of the seal hunt, the
whale hunt, and other scenes of village life. A friendly nurse provided more suitable paper, ordered Christmas cards, and launched
him on a career which has made his finely drawn scenes of Eskimo

An Eskimo drum maker in Nome

life familiar to many Alaskans. For many years he worked as a roofer and in other trades. But now he makes a modest living as an artist. He built his home in an Anchorage suburb by a barter system, exchanging his drawings on reindeer skin which he processes himself for the labor and materials provided by a contractor.

On the other hand, some of the craftsmen and women have had

St. Lawrence Islanders drilling ivory

difficult going in recent years. The Nome Skin Sewers Co-operative Association got off to a fine start. Admiral Richard E. Byrd
and his men went to the South Pole in parkas and mukluks made
by these women and left them a bonus in 1936 to set up their
co-operative. The garments are designed in a big ramshackle
wooden shop on a Nome side street; most of the actual work is
done by the women in their homes.

But the Association's business has fallen off in recent years.
"We just can't provide work any more," says Mrs. Emma Willoya,
the manager. Competition from machine-made garments is appar-
ently one factor, inadequate promotion another.

A competent, articulate Eskimo woman who received two Presi-
dential citations for her work as an OPA volunteer during and after
World War II, Mrs. Willoya sees unemployment as the biggest

A native with his reindeer

problem of her people in the Nome area. Her husband has been a longshoreman for some years but has been getting very little work.

"My husband used to have one of the largest reindeer herds in the North," she says.

"What happened?"

"The wolves got most of them. Two-legged wolves got the rest."

Depletion of the reindeer herds has been a major problem. While the wolves may have been largely responsible, some Eskimos also blame white businessmen who went into reindeer herding commercially. The government now restricts use of the reindeer to the natives, but the herds are still below their former size. The missing reindeer are symptomatic of the difficulties of continuing this way of life under modern conditions.

Many Alaskans believe that eventually the Arctic and Bering Sea areas will be built up, that oil and coal and mining will supplement the old fishing and hunting activities. Both from their own experiences and from the explorations, studies, and writings of Vilhjalmur Stefansson and others, they have come to realize that man can adapt himself to the Arctic and make use of its natural riches. They see the possibility of a modern economy in the Arctic in which the Eskimo will play a leading role. Development of the resources of Alaska will help solve the problems of the Eskimos, as it will of the Indians and the Aleuts. This will make it possible for them to use the skills they acquire at Mt. Edgecumbe and to take advantage of the benefits of education. The general trend seems to be toward integration of the native population in the general life of Alaska rather than toward separation. Thus, we may be confident that the native peoples will play their role in the building up of Alaska; and they will advance as Alaska moves forward.

5: The Battle for Statehood

It was warm and sunny over most of Alaska the evening of June 30, 1958. It was one of those nights of the midnight sun in the North. But this was a particular night for celebration. Everywhere there was dancing in the streets. Flags were unfurled. Sirens sounded. A big bonfire burned in Nome on the beach facing Russia across the Bering Sea. In Anchorage the bonfire was bigger, as befits Alaska's largest city. There was also a 49-gun salute from the 207th Infantry Battalion of the Alaska National Guard. In the capital, Juneau, a big bell, modeled after the Liberty Bell in Philadelphia, chimed forty-nine times. In Fairbanks a giant gold star floated from the top of the tallest building, a modern elevator apartment hotel, and the Chena River in the heart of the city ran golden for a short while with artificial dye.

Participants in the celebrations, men and women, wore summer clothes much as did men and women everywhere else in the United States that evening. They didn't know that back in Washington, D.C. several United States senators had just finished explaining that it was freezing in Alaska. They didn't much care either. For the Senate had ignored the colorful descriptions of Alaska's frozen wastes. It had voted 64 to 20 to admit Alaska as the forty-ninth state. It had removed the final important barrier to Alaska statehood.

Alaska's status as a subordinate territory of the United States began and ended with a discussion of the weather. Shortly after the 1867 purchase, Rep. Benjamin F. Loan, Missouri Republican, said that "the acquisition of this inhospitable and barren waste would never add a dollar to the wealth of our country or furnish any homes to our people." Virtually the same points were made in the Senate in 1958. Senators John C. Stennis and James O. Eastland, both of Mississippi, orated at some length about the uninhabitable Alaskan climate. Senator Richard B. Russell, Georgia Democrat, told the Senate that nobody wanted to live in Alaska. He predicted that without large-scale military spending "there would be left only a few hardy souls and Eskimos." Russell also predicted that statehood would lead to "a hegira of people out of Alaska" because of high taxes.

For the ninety-one years in between, Alaska's supposedly impossible climate was discussed in endless pages of the Congressional Record and of official reports. Early in the day, people in Alaska began to suspect the good faith of some of the self-appointed meteorological experts who were always proving that the territory was one big iceberg. In 1885, Alfred P. Swineford, Alaska's second governor, suggested a motive. He said that "paid agents" of the Alaska Commercial Company were making "a studied and determined effort . . . to imbue the general public, as well as the government, with the belief that there is nothing of value in Alaska save its fur-bearing animals." The company, he explained, was "defeating nearly every proposed settlement and development of Alaska" so that it could maintain its monopoly on the Pribilof seal islands and keep out competition. And he charged that company agents and even some government officials "broadcast statements concerning the climate and undeveloped resources of Alaska which they knew were utterly false."

With the passing of the years, different private corporations and government officials were identified by Alaskans as the villains in the drama, and the Alaskans themselves made varying demands for self-government until they finally united behind statehood. But the alignment and the issues remained much the same. On one side were interests with a substantial stake in Alaska who preferred

Alaska's first Mayor and City Council, 1901.

Bill McPhee   John Harris   S.H.Stevens   Charlie Hoxsie
Tex Rickard   Julius Guise   Capt. Geiger
Mayor

to maintain that stake by keeping the territory locked up to potential competitors. They felt this could best be achieved by having Alaska ruled from Washington. On the other side was a constantly growing majority of Alaskans who looked forward to the development of the area and who believed that this could only be done by a greater measure of self-government and representation in Washington.

Juneau miners began clamoring for self-government for Alaska in the early 1880's soon after Joe Juneau and Richard Harris made the first big gold strike. The clamor grew considerably at the height of the gold rush at the turn of the century. But there was little response from Washington. Sometimes Alaskans got impatient.

In 1905 the people of Valdez, despairing that Congress would ever enact the pending bill to give Alaska an elected delegate to Congress, passed this resolution: "On behalf of 60,000 American citizens in Alaska who are denied the right of representation in any form, we demand, in mass meeting assembled, that Alaska be annexed to Canada." The newspapers in Canada's Yukon Territory taunted the United States, noting that this was a "deliciously refreshing demonstration of how far Congress had departed" from original American principles. For several years in Valdez, Seward, and Fairbanks there were citizens who thought Canada might be more disposed to grant Alaskans first-class citizenship. But essentially this was a move to put pressure on Washington, and Congress did in 1906 finally decide to let Alaska have an elected but voteless delegate.

For a generation Alaska politics was defined in terms of "the Guggs vs. the Wicks." The Guggs were supporters of the Guggenheim-Morgan interests who in 1906 formed the Alaska Syndicate which controlled much of the area's economy. The Wicks were supporters of that fabulous Alaskan James Wickersham. Wickersham was a lawyer, a judge, a student of ethnology, geology, and geography, an outdoors man and mountain climber, author of the definitive bibliography on Alaska, and above all, a battler for Alaska statehood.

In 1900 President McKinley appointed Wickersham a judge in Alaska's third district. He built the first Alaska courthouse of logs in the little mining town of Eagle, traveling through his territory by dog-sled. He endeared himself to Alaskans by holding court in Nome and cleaning out the mess created there by the corrupt Judge Noyes who favored the outside claim-jumpers. But Wickersham was less popular in the United States Senate, where his appointment was blocked for seven successive years. President Theodore Roosevelt got around the road-block by giving him continued recess appointments. Elected as Alaska's Delegate to Congress in 1908, Wickersham rallied Alaskans to the cause of a representative territorial government—and against the Guggenheim interests which opposed the extension of self-government to Alaska.

James Wickersham

The passage of the Organic Act of Alaska in 1912, granting Alaska limited territorial status, was in large measure the achievement of Wickersham and the forces supporting him. The act gave Alaska a legislature, but not an elected governor. The Constitution and laws of the United States were extended to the Territory; but

One of the first locomotives on the Alaska Railroad
contrasted with a new, modern train

Alaska was not permitted to establish its own judiciary or law
enforcement system. Nor was it allowed to regulate the salmon canneries which remained under federal jurisdiction. While it was
grudgingly given power to tax the canneries, the canners could,
and did, refuse to pay the taxes. Wickersham also fathered the
legislation, passed in 1915, authorizing the building of a government railroad in Alaska which was completed in 1923. The railroad, connecting Seward and Fairbanks and 470 miles long, was a
historic step forward.

The bill of 1912 was only a stepping stone for Wickersham and
his supporters. As early as 1910, he had written an article for
Collier's entitled "The State of Alaska: The Forty-Ninth Star." In
1916 he introduced the first statehood bill. But statehood was still

A streamliner of the Alaska Railroad

a long way off. The next two decades were to be a period of stagnation for Alaska—in both the economic and political spheres. Its legislature and delegate in Congress were engaged in continuing guerilla warfare designed to win full territorial status without the restrictions of the Organic Law of 1912 and to regulate the fisheries which were depleting Alaska's salmon resources.

While President Franklin D. Roosevelt showed more interest in Alaska than some of his predecessors, the only move of lasting importance during his Administration was the founding of the Matanuska agricultural colony in 1935. Farmers were in trouble all over the United States, and the idea occurred to Roosevelt, Harry Hopkins, and other government officials of helping some of them settle in Alaska. The fertile Matanuska Valley, about fifty miles from Anchorage, was picked for an experiment in subsistence

Laborers arriving in Palmer to begin construction of facilities
in Matanuska Valley

farming. Two hundred families were resettled there. It was rough
going at first. Scarlet fever, measles, and chicken pox epidemics
spread among the children. Heavy windstorms devastated some of
the early tent homes. The colony was severely attacked by critics
of the Roosevelt New Deal, and it is undoubtedly true that some
mistakes were made. Not all the colonists selected by relief officials
were experienced farmers. The subsistence farming concept had
to be abandoned later in favor of regular commercial farms. But
the project was a major advance for Alaska because it established
agriculture for the first time on a firm footing. The Matanuska
Valley settlement became a self-sustaining agricultural community.
It showed that Alaska had fine soil suitable for farming—specif-
ically, for dairying, vegetable farming, hog raising and poultry.

Laborers cutting trees and clearing the land

It remained, however, not for the New Deal but for World War II to rediscover Alaska and its aspirations for statehood. As the war focused increased attention on Alaska, Delegate Anthony Dimond introduced a statehood bill in 1943, 27 years after Wickersham's first effort in this direction. Delegate E. L. Bartlett introduced the next statehood bills in 1945 and 1947. The latter Bartlett bill was significant chiefly because it was the first Alaska statehood measure on which congressional hearings were held. The bill also had behind it the authority of a 1946 referendum of Alaska voters which favored statehood.

The Washington hearings showed growing support for statehood. General of the Air Force, H. H. Arnold, came out for statehood at the hearings. So did Secretary of the Interior Julius A. Krug, whose testimony touched on what many Alaskans felt was the crux of the matter. "Alaska," he said, "has suffered for many years under what is virtually a colonial system that has encouraged absentee exploitation of its natural resources. . . . If Alaska is granted statehood, its people will have more to say about their economic as well as their political destiny. Absentee interests, working for their special ends, will find it more difficult to dominate the economy of the area."

The hearings were enlivened by a charge from James A. Wooten, president of Alaska Airlines, that representatives of the canned salmon industry threatened to withdraw their business if he didn't stop supporting statehood. The fact is that Wooten's air line did lose the rather substantial business of transporting cannery workers and fishermen. A Ketchikan newspaper publisher was similarly penalized by a loss of advertising revenue.

While the Alaska statehood bill got unanimous committee approval, it never reached the House floor. It died in a Rules Committee pigeonhole—mainly because of opposition from Southern Representatives. For the next decade Alaska got the legislative "runaround." In 1950 the House passed statehood bills for both Alaska and Hawaii, but the measures were killed in the Senate. In 1952 statehood lost in the Senate by only one vote. In 1954 the Senate finally did approve statehood for both territories—but this time the House bottled up the bills.

It seemed difficult to explain the repeated rebuffs for statehood. Support kept mounting, and the opposition became less formidable. The Democratic Party platform in 1948 came out for immediate statehood, the Republicans for eventual statehood. In 1952 both party conventions endorsed immediate statehood. Hearings disclosed backing from the United States Chamber of Commerce, the CIO, AFL, American Legion, Veterans of Foreign Wars, Catholic War Veterans, National Grange, General Federation of Women's Clubs, and many other powerful organizations. Prominent military figures spoke up for statehood. Somewhat later the oil industry quietly put its influence behind statehood, on the assumption that this would open Alaska for economic development.

In 1951 a Senate committee reported that there was little opposition to statehood within Alaska and that "the burden was carried by representatives of the fish-packing industry with headquarters in the states." The arguments against statehood were stale and shopworn. Alaska's small population was cited repeatedly, but was refuted by citing the population statistics of other territories admitted as states. The weather in Alaska was again a favorite topic of congressional oratory. Senator Stennis of Mississippi banged on his desk for emphasis as he read and re-read a newspaper article containing the sentence: "Brief exposure can mean death." The arguments were not in themselves persuasive. But the cause of statehood had become entangled in a new labyrinth of obstacles.

Southern senators, who had suddenly rediscovered that Alaska was cold, were more concerned about the likelihood that Alaska and Hawaii would elect senators opposed to racialism and the white supremacy position and to unlimited Dixie filibusters. Republicans worried that Alaska would elect a Democratic congressional delegation. Democrats feared that Hawaii would go Republican. Statehood for the two territories became a political football. President Eisenhower, who had been for immediate statehood before his election in 1952, reversed himself in 1953. Although many leading military figures favored statehood, Secretary of Defense Charles E. Wilson declared it "in the interests of the national security" for Alaska to remain a territory.

As the issue appeared deadlocked, the next move came from the embattled Alaskans. At the suggestion of a friendly New Orleans businessman, they looked into their history books and read up on the Tennessee Plan. This was the device by which Tennessee in 1791 elected two senators prior to admission to the union and sent them riding on horseback to the national capital. Other territories in a hurry to become states: Michigan, California, Oregon, and Kansas, had used the same plan. Alaskans decided to bury old differences, unite forces, and act as if their territory was already in fact a state.

Alaska duly elected delegates to a constitutional convention in 1955. The delegates drafted a state constitution which was approved by a decisive two-to-one vote in 1956. Then in October of that year the voters sent two "senators" and one "representative" to Washington. The "congressional" delegation toured the country in a statehood caravan, picking up support as it went. In Washington it acted as a potent lobby for statehood. Backing up these efforts inside Alaska was an organization called "Operation Statehood," which raised funds, issued publicity, and put pressure on Congress.

It was getting more and more difficult to argue that Alaskans didn't really want statehood. There had, it is true, long been a minority of Alaskans opposed to statehood. Some were described by critics as political descendants of the "Guggs"—that is, spokesmen for outside interests with a stake in maintaining the *status quo*. Some were businessmen who had established local monopolies they did not want to see challenged by competitors. Local jealousies played a role. Juneau feared that statehood would mean shifting the capital to Anchorage or Fairbanks. There were sincere fears among many that statehood would impose too heavy a tax burden and that Alaska was not economically prepared for statehood. These fears persisted to some degree until the very end. But, as the 1956 vote on the state constitution showed, the opposition to statehood represented a constantly dwindling minority. Moreover, it was for the most part a minority torn by doubts rather than a convinced, crusading, lobbying opposition.

The last big push began in 1957. Both Senate and House committees approved statehood bills. Representative Howard Smith of Virginia, chairman of the House Rules Committee, stalled the bill for almost a year. Important compromises had to be made to get action. In time of military emergency the President was given power to withdraw from the new state a substantial area in the northern part of Alaska. A special and unprecedented provision in the statehood bill put control of the fisheries under the federal government—although every one of the other states has control of its own fisheries. But Alaskans swallowed their disappointment and rallied behind the bill. Finally, the House approved the measure and on June 30, 1958, the Senate acted. The last steps, approval by the President and ratification by the voters, were only a matter of form. The vote this time was five to one for statehood.

Alaska had enormous assets as it became the forty-ninth state: solid support from its own population, nation-wide good will, tremendous natural resources and increased interest in their ex-

The governor's mansion in Juneau

ploitation. Its streamlined 1956 constitution, considered one of the
most advanced in the United States, is ready for operation. The
state legislature meets once a year. The governor has sweeping
powers. The constitution adopts the "strong executive" concept.
Discrimination against any person because of race or color is
banned—a safeguard for the native population. The constitution
pays a tribute to youth. The voting age is 19.

All Alaska has celebrated the victory, and is prepared to reap
its benefits. But the job is just beginning for the new state. Alaska
has to build a judicial and penal system from scratch. There has
been no system of territorial courts staffed and operated by Alaskans. Virtually all legal business has had to be handled by four
federal district courts. The system, set up some fifty years ago,
was not very effective then. It has not improved with passing
decades. It has meant bogging down the four federal judges and

the Circuit Court of Appeals in San Francisco with petty Alaska cases that didn't belong in a federal court to begin with. Prisoners had to be shipped to the mainland. There were no territorial prisons. Juneau's federal jail, an imposing nineteenth-century wooden structure suitable for a museum, is the town joke. By now the courts are far behind in their case load. It will take years for the mess to be cleared up.

Other branches of the territorial government, however, have gradually been built up over the years, and in this sense Alaska is quite well prepared for statehood. The men elected in the Democratic sweep of November 1958 have all had long and extensive experience. For governor, the voters picked William A. Egan who at 44 has been airplane pilot, cannery worker, truck driver and grocer. At the 1955–56 Constitutional Convention, he helped smooth differences and cement agreement behind the program which provided a major impetus to statehood. Elected senator at 71 was Ernest Gruening, a grizzled veteran of the fight for statehood. Trained as a physician, Gruening turned newspaperman and for a time was editor of the *Nation* magazine. He was appointed Governor of Alaska in 1939 and served 14 years, playing a major role in the postwar build-up of Alaska. Few men have contributed more to Alaskan statehood. Senator Edward Lewis Bartlett, a one-time gold miner and journalist, had at 54 served 14 years as Alaska's delegate in Congress. He introduced statehood bills back in the '40s and helped pave the way for congressional acceptance of statehood. Alaska's lone congressman, 55-year-old Ralph J. Rivers, was a former attorney general of the Territory and a former mayor of Fairbanks. Along with Gruening and Egan, he was a member of Alaska's "Tennessee Plan" delegation to Congress which toured the United States for statehood. These men and their associates are no novices.

But there remains the complex problem of streamlining a rather unwieldy, jerry-built apparatus and eliminating overlapping functions of state and federal governments. There is the urgent question of taxation to support a state government. There is the increased responsibility of the new state to its native population. Above all, there is the long-range problem of developing the economic policies which will help Alaska grow and realize the potential of its vast natural resources. Even as they celebrated their formal entry into the Union—on January 3, 1959—serious-minded Alaskans were well aware of the many tasks ahead.

6: Unlocking the Treasure

"What does statehood mean for Alaska?" Ben Crawford, president of the City National Bank of Anchorage and of several other financial institutions, repeats the question. Then he says slowly, "Well, there are two big things. First it gives us first-class citizenship. Second, it eliminates some of the economic discriminations that have held us back. Some of our hopes and dreams can now come to realization."

Crawford is typical of the young men who are taking over in Alaska. Born of pioneer parents who came to the Anchorage area in 1899, he has infinite faith in the new state's possibilities. At 39 he is the head of several other financial institutions besides the bank and a director of a score of community and civic organizations. He was also a leader in the fight for statehood, and the reasons he gives for backing statehood are typical of those cited by other businessmen throughout Alaska. In fact, they are the same reasons cited by labor leaders, public officials, and just plain citizens.

Ask them about the impact of statehood and they will talk about roads, steamship transportation, fisheries, land policy. They will talk mainly economics. They believe that the withholding of first-class citizenship doomed their economy to stagnation. They say that lack of representation resulted in failure to develop many of Alaska's resources and in senseless exploitation of others by absentee owners, often protected by special-interest legislation in Washington. All this, they are now convinced, has begun to change, and will change still more in the decade ahead.

C. W. Snedden, publisher of the *Fairbanks News-Miner* which was a vigorous voice of the statehood movement, cites several helpful consequences of the victory in Washington. One of them is partly personal. "Statehood," he says, "means repeal of the Jones Act, and that means a saving of $17.60 a ton on newsprint for the *News-Miner*." But Snedden is only one of thousands of Alaska businessmen who will gain from elimination of the Jones Act— named after Senator Wesley L. Jones of Washington. In fact, all of Alaska is expected to benefit from a resulting drop in high transportation costs.

The Jones Act, Snedden explains, consists of only two words— "excluding Alaska." Senator Jones had the two words inserted in the Merchant Marine Act of 1920. The meaning of the two words was that freight between Canada and Alaska had to be shipped on American bottoms. The result is that goods from close-by Canadian ports were sent first to Seattle and then trans-shipped on American vessels—usually those of the Alaska Steamship Company, which has long enjoyed a virtual monopoly of steamship traffic in the new state.

A 1946 Congressional hearing showed that steamship rates on many commodities between Seattle and Alaska—less than 900 miles—were two or three times higher than the rates between San Francisco and Honolulu—just under 2,400 miles. The same hearings showed that it cost $1.44 to ship a davenport by rail 906 miles from San Francisco to Seattle—and $11.34 by steamship from Seattle to Juneau, which is not much farther by water. Alaskans complain of all kinds of discriminatory steamship rates. An airline executive in Juneau says that it costs him more to get parts from Seattle than it does to get the same parts in Anchorage, which is several hundred miles more distant. Salmon canneries, frequently linked by common ownership with the steamship interests, have received favored rates compared with other industries or the general population. A high official of the Alaska territorial government quipped shortly before the change-over to statehood:

It was hard getting appropriations for roads

"They're charging us more and more for hauling less and less."

Repeal of the Jones Act is expected to end the monopoly of the Alaska Steamship Company, introduce some competition into the shipping industry, and result in lower rates. This is extraordinarily important for Alaska, which relies on steamship transportation for its food, its consumers goods, and its industrial equipment. The Alaska Resource Development Board has described "high transportation costs" as "one of the principal obstacles to the development" of the area. The Jones Act has been an important factor in keeping these costs high.

"We need roads," says Al Anderson, executive director of the Development Board. "We need roads very badly. We had to go to Congress with hat in hand to get roads. Now we are assured of a proportionate share of the money."

This sums up another effect of statehood, and one, which like

Alaska has less than 523 miles of railroad track

repeal of the Jones Act, will go a long way toward breaking Alaska's transportation bottleneck.

Alaska had virtually no adequate roads until World War II forced the military into a major road-building program—principally the Alaska Highway with a few connecting links with major Alaska cities. The post-war defense program boosted federal spending for Alaska to an all-time high of $30,600,000 in 1950, but by 1955 appropriations had dropped to $10,000,000. The galling thing to Alaskans was that they had been excluded from participation in the Federal Highway Program since its enactment in 1916. As recently as 1955, Congress provided that the Alaska quota for federal highway funds be based on one third of its area. Even the

(Left) Railroad and dock facilities at Seward, and (right)
the Alaska Railroad crossing Hurricane Gulch

Federal Highway Act of 1956 did little to remedy the glaring in-
equality of treatment. The argument was that the vastness of
Alaska's area barred a proportionate share of the funds. Ignored
was the counterargument that Alaska's need for roads was equally
vast.

Alaska's facilities for land transportation are extremely limited,
so limited in fact that more expensive air transport has been used
for much light freight. Even buses and gold-mining equipment
have been delivered by air. The government-owned Alaska Railroad has 470 miles of track on its main line from Seward to Fairbanks, and 67 miles of branch road. There are about 5,000 miles
of road inside Alaska—a 2,000-mile network of primary routes
and a 3,200-mile secondary system. Many areas have neither railroad nor road facilities. Juneau, Petersburg, Wrangell, and Ketchikan are among the southeast Alaska cities which have been press-
ing for direct road connections with the U.S., and Nome has been
campaigning for a road to connect it with the interior. While no
immediate extension of the Alaska Railroad is in prospect, expansion of the road system would go a long way toward giving Alaska

(Left) Unloading humpback and dog salmon caught by seine
at False Pass Cannery, and (right) brailing a floating
salmon trap in Southeast Alaska

a better transportation system. Even the present highway system
has resulted in the development of a sizable trucking industry. More
roads combined with lower steamship rates and modern shipping
and packaging methods may eventually bring some significant re-
ductions in Alaska's transportation costs.

Publisher Robert B. Atwood of the *Anchorage Daily Times*
says, "Statehood will give us a fighting chance to save our salmon
from destruction by fish traps. Present conservation laws are for
conservation of canners. We're for conservation of fish."

Control of the fisheries has been one of the great stakes in the
battle of statehood. Fishing and canning rather than mining has
constituted Alaska's biggest industry. From 1867 to 1950, more
than $2,000,000,000 worth of fish products was extracted from
Alaskan waters, salmon alone accounting for better than 90 percent of the total. The industry now does about a $90,000,000
yearly business and employs about 25,000 workers.

Purse seining for salmon in Yes Bay—the most common way
of capturing fish

But it is an industry that has had violent ups and downs, and in
recent years the trend has been straight down. The canned salmon
pack in 1957 was less than half that of the annual pack during
the 'twenties. Fishermen and cannery workers have been unable to
make a living as this seasonal industry has kept skidding. Alaskans
blame the decline not so much on the natural habits of the salmon
as on the practices of the canners. They blame particularly the
salmon trap, a floating or stationary mechanical device which effec-
tively barricades a stream and catches all the salmon on their way
to spawn. They believe that the fish traps, owned largely by the
cannery interests in Seattle and on the West Coast, have been
responsible for the drop in the salmon catch and for the difficult
economic conditions of Alaska's independent fishermen.

This whole issue is charged with bitterness built up over the

A floating fish trap

years. When Alaskans condemn "absentee owners," they are usually talking about the fish canning industry (that is, when they
are not talking about the Alaska Steamship Company). They condemn the industry for importing a large portion of its workers,
thus depriving many Alaskans of work. They assert that it has
evaded taxes, that it has exerted powerful pressure in Washington
against proper conservation practices, against statehood, against
opening up Alaska for economic development.

It is against this background that the united demand of Alaskans
for abolishing the salmon traps and for state control of fisheries
has assumed such emotional as well as economic significance.
Many Alaskans believe that the Fish and Wildlife Service, con-

tinuing the functions of the U.S. Bureau of Fisheries has done a poor conservation job, that it has been subjected to too much pressure from the canners, and that it just hasn't been close enough to the situation. They believe that only state control can cope with the situation. In this connection they cite the position of the conservationist Izaak Walton League in favor of state control of fisheries.

Statehood has given the Alaskans new leverage in their long battle. On the eve of the 1958 elections in Alaska, Secretary of the Interior Fred Seaton acted to ban the fish traps. But administrative orders could, of course, be reversed. So Alaskans are resolved to continue the fight until their state government wins full control of the fisheries. As if in response to this determination, Governor-elect William A. Egan moved swiftly to redeem one of his election campaign pledges. On January 5, 1959, he ordered the discontinuance of licensing of the highly controversial fishing traps. His move was widely supported throughout Alaska.

Senator Ernest Gruening, a Democrat, says, "One of the greatest benefits of statehood is that it will make at least a share of our abundant land available for use." Publisher Snedden, a Republican, says, "No access to the land is our biggest problem."

Statehood means that the new state government will control about a fifth of Alaska's vast acreage and will in turn make it available for private ownership and use. Here is the biggest stake of all in statehood—exploitation of Alaska's hidden wealth.

The startling fact is that private ownership of land has been almost nonexistent in Alaska: 99.99 of the land has been owned by the federal government. Some public lands have been leased for private development. But many millions of acres are barred from any private use by federal withdrawals and reservations. Historically there have been innumerable restrictions against doing anything with Alaska's seemingly limitless acreage.

In other frontier areas, squatters' rights prevailed. Settlers got land on a first-come, first-served basis. But Gruening emphasizes that in Alaska the Interior Department barred attempts to make land claims as contrary to law. General land legislation, supposedly easing the situation, was passed at the end of the last century. But

Logging and felling in South Tongass National Forest

even then absence of government surveys virtually cancelled out the effect of the liberalizing enactment. A further step was taken with the passage of the Alaska Public Sale Act in 1949. Yet homesteading and acquisition of farm land have remained far more difficult in Alaska than elsewhere, despite the apparent availability of hundreds of millions of acres of unused land.

Use of Alaska's natural resources was severely limited. For years there was a flat ban on the cutting of timber from public lands. There was a notable case in Alaska's early years of a salmon cannery in Klawock which built a sawmill to pack its products in barrels and boxes—but was required to ship its fish in imported barrels and boxes. For years export of lumber to the states was prohibited—a restriction which did not displease the Northwest

Cordova, May 4, 1911: Dumping foreign coal into the bay

lumber interests. Lumber could be used and shipped locally, but high steamship rates made this rather impractical.

Land use in Alaska was restricted for a variety of reasons. To begin with, there was just plain neglect, similar to the oversight that denied Alaska any kind of government or law for seventeen years. Then the influence of private interests such as the Alaska Commercial Company was brought to bear against opening up Alaska to competitive development. A major part in locking up Alaska was, however, played in the early 1900's by the conservationists, who had the very best of motives. They were concerned partly with preserving Alaska as a wilderness area, partly with preventing its ruthless exploitation by corporate monopolies.

These conservationists rose up in protest at the turn of the century against what they believed were attempts by monopoly interests to use fraudulent means to capture control of Alaska's coal resources. They charged that coal leases were obtained by these interests in the name of dummies. There was undoubtedly fraud involved in these and other cases. Evidence was shown, for example,

Cordova as it looks today

that the Alaska Syndicate defrauded the government of $50,000 in a coal contract deal, and there were charges that Attorney General George Wickersham was shielding and defending the Syndicate. But the remedy chosen by the conservationists, led by Gifford Pinchot, was to invalidate all coal leases and to withdraw from use all coal lands in the public domain.

The Alaskans protested bitterly. In 1911 the citizens of Cordova staged a repeat of the Boston Tea Party, dumping into their harbor the coal they had to import from Canada instead of mining their own. Senator Thomas J. Walsh, a supporter of conservation who later exposed the Teapot Dome oil scandal, said that the original withdrawal of the coal lands was warranted but that "to have kept that great wealth locked up . . . for a period of eight years approached in gravity to a crime."

The controversy over the coal leases split the Republican Party wide open, and was a principal factor in the formation of Theodore Roosevelt's Progressive Party in 1912. The conservationists certainly succeeded in briefly putting Alaska in the limelight. But, despite their high-mindedness, they also prevented its development for a considerable period. The restrictions they imposed not only stifled coal mining but slowed up other attempts to extract Alaska's mineral resources. The point of view of the more extreme conservationists was expressed as recently as 1940 by the late Robert Marshall, an official of the Forestry Service, who said that Alaska should "remain primarily a great reservoir of resources, largely untapped at present, but available for future use."

Whatever the intention, the result of the conservationist crusade was to conserve some of Alaska's resources by locking them up against any use. The trouble has been that some resources, such as fish and seals, were wantonly destroyed, while others have been withheld altogether. Moreover, one actual effect of the restrictions on land use was to perpetuate and strengthen those monopolies already in the field, such as the Alaska Syndicate, the Alaska Steamship Company, and the salmon cannery interests. Thus, the net effect of government policy was to hinder Alaska's development.

Victorious advocates of statehood maintain that they have not the slightest intention of scuttling conservation practices—and, particularly in the case of salmon, they claim that they will be more zealous than the federal government in conserving natural resources.

In any case, the federal government will turn over to the new state about a quarter of Alaska's land area; the rest will remain under federal ownership and control. More than 100,000,000 acres are becoming state property and are being made available for private settlement and use to settlers, farmers, businessmen, and industry. This acreage—larger than the total area of California— can be a substantial factor in fostering economic growth.

At the opposite pole from the more extreme conservationists were the private interests which opposed any restrictions on the exploitation of Alaska's wealth. Now the issue becomes whether it is possible to make Alaska's resources available for economic development without squandering and destroying them. Statehood removes some of the discriminations and limitations that have held Alaska back in the past. But one of the responsibilities it imposes is to develop safeguards against reckless exploitation of Alaska's wealth. Alaskans realize this as they take their first forward steps within the Union.

7: The New Klondike

In his stories of the days of the Klondike gold strike, Jack London did more than perhaps any other writer to perpetuate the myth of Alaska as a battleground of gallant men and dogs against the unconquerable forces of nature. But London also had a vision of new days coming, of an Alaska at last subdued by man. In a little-known magazine article written in 1900 shortly after his return from the Yukon, he prophesied a new Klondike, an industrialized Alaska in which the romance of the primitive would yield to modern industry:

The new Klondike, the Klondike of the future, will present remarkable contrasts with the Klondike of the past. Natural obstacles will be cleared away or surmounted, primitive methods abandoned, and the hardship of toil and travel reduced to the smallest possible minimum. Exploration and transportation will be systematized. There will be no waste energy, no harum-scarum carrying on industry. The frontiersman will yield to the laborer, the prospector to the mining engineer, the dog-driver to the engine-driver, the trader and speculator to the steady-going modern man of business; for these are the men in whose hands the destiny of the Klondike will be intrusted.

Alaska now stands on the threshold of that new Klondike. Much of what London wrote has already come to pass. The frontiersman is being replaced by the laborer, the prospector by the mining engineer, the dog-driver not so much by the engine-driver as by the airplane pilot, the speculator by the investor, the merchant, the banker. Alaska still has a long way to go. The primitive and the backward still intrude on the new and the modern. But even the visionary London would have been overwhelmed by some of what is happening now, just beginning to happen—with much more to come. New riches are being prospected, but in a way he never could have imagined.

Prospectors are now hunting for black gold, for oil—in planes and helicopters. These include private firms as well as government departments. A fleet of 55 helicopters has been flying out of the Anchorage area over the Kenai Peninsula with cameras and electro-magnetic detectors. The aerial prospecting paid off when skilled crews moved in to determine whether there actually was oil in the promising geological formations. July 27, 1957, was a big day in Alaska industry. Talk of oil became a reality. Richfield Oil Corporation sank a well on the Kenai Moose Range, then announced that production tests disclosed it was capable of flowing at a rate of 900 barrels of petroleum a day. Geologists indicate that there may be a reserve of one billion barrels in that oil field alone.

There has been talk of oil in Alaska for more than a century. Oil seeps on the Alaska Peninsula were discovered even before the Seward purchase in 1867. The first samples were taken in 1882, and were promising. Sporadic digging was undertaken. But not much was done about it except by the United States Navy, which after World War II explored extensively for oil in the far north and found it. The Navy has set up Naval Petroleum Reserve No. 4 in the Arctic coastal plain area; it contains at least two oil fields and two gas fields.

Oil corporations also undertook extensive exploration work following the war. But it was the Richfield strike that set off a serious oil boom. Millions of acres of potential oil lands are now under lease, with applications pending for millions more. The major oil companies have set aside about $100,000,000 for oil exploration in Alaska. Humble, Shell, Standard of California, Phillips are all in the picture. There is hardly a major section of Alaska which is exempt from the rapidly developing oil boom. "The whole Yukon basin may be a huge oil field," says a Fairbanks businessman.

Farthest north pipeline in the world, it carries oil for fuel for
the Army from the port of Haines to Fairbanks

The Alaska oil boom could revolutionize the entire state. Already
oil leases are producing substantial revenues for a state government
which needs them badly to start functioning smoothly. If preliminary drilling is followed by large-scale operations, tens of millions
of dollars will have to be spent on new facilities, on roads and pipelines. There would be a need for thousands of oil workers. Already
there has been talk of building refineries in Alaska, and this would
give the new state a major manufacturing industry which in turn
would lead to subsidiary industries. It would also make possible a
big reduction in the high cost of transportation by auto and truck.

A gold dredge near Fairbanks

Regular gas in the Fairbanks area sells for about 50 cents a gallon, and it is often more expensive along the road.

Another major development has been the opening up for commercial use of part of the Gubik gas field 450 miles north of Fairbanks where the Navy discovered natural gas. A company was formed in Fairbanks, largely with Alaska capital, to begin preliminary development of this area. It has plans to lay a pipeline to Fairbanks and possibly also to Anchorage. The result would be to cut down Alaska's big fuel bill for both business and consumer use and to pave the way for further industrialization, which has been impeded by the lack of cheap power and fuel.

All this is just beginning. Morgan J. Davis, president of the Humble Oil Company, told the Anchorage Chamber of Commerce at a banquet in 1958 that Alaska is "still a tenderfoot—still a cheechako—in comparison with other oil-producing states." He

A tin mine in the Port Clarence district showing the special
insulation used against severe winter weather

noted that up through the end of 1957 only 109 exploratory wells
had been dug in all Alaska over a 57-year period, whereas in the
Gulf Coast area there are currently "more than three times that
many wildcats drilled in a single month." It may take years for
large-scale commercial oil production to materialize. But Alaska is
at least at the start of the long road to becoming a major oil-
producing state.

Alaska's riches in mineral deposits are almost unlimited. "We
have copper, lead, nickel, zinc, chrome, mercury, tin, coal, bauxite,
uranium and many others," says Waino Hendrickson, Alaska's acting governor before statehood became a reality. "Alaska will be a
mining country again."

Hendrickson didn't even mention gold, although in dollar value
there is still more gold mined than any other mineral, about

Surface plant of a coal mine

$8,000,000 a year. Lode mining has been abandoned, but there are still big gold dredges at work at Nome and Fairbanks. These are operated by the United States Smelting, Refining, and Mining Company, a Boston corporation which has been the major gold-producing outfit in Alaska for many years. But gold mining is declining and is probably on its way out. The Boston company announced in 1958 that it was planning to discontinue its dredging at Nome. The fixed price of gold at $35 an ounce, contrasted with rising production costs, provides the answer. Alaska still has the gold. But the government has all it needs for the foreseeable future at Fort Knox. Not even the most optimistic Alaskans are willing to predict a rise in the price of gold, and it is the baser metals on which the interest of twentieth-century prospectors is now focused.

In 1955 Don and Jan Ross, a husband and wife team, were flying aerial reconnaissance in a Piper Cub over southeast Alaska looking for uranium. They thought they detected some on Prince of Wales Island with their nucleometer. Closer examination and testing showed they were right. Climax Molybdenum, a major United States metals firm, signed a contract with the Rosses for exploration and began test drilling. In 1957 Climax started shipping uranium ore from Alaska.

Probably the most important untapped mineral resources in Alaska are coal, iron ore, tin, and copper. Of these only coal is being mined now to any degree; coal mining has been running at a rate of about $6,000,000 a year. There has been some interest recently in stepping up coal production, and Japanese business groups are thinking in terms of developing a major source of coking coal in Alaska. The high production cost is now the principal obstacle to development of Alaska's coal resources. If this could be overcome, the old anomaly of importing coal to a coal-rich country would be ended, and Alaska would have a major source of cheap power.

Although there is little copper being mined now, the potential is at least suggested by the $227,000,000 in copper extracted in a 25-year period, mainly from the Kennecott mines of the Guggenheim-Morgan interests. Alaska's tin deposits are attracting increased attention because the United States has virtually no tin of its own and is dependent on the resources of Bolivia, Malaya, and Indonesia. There is plenty of iron ore in Alaska, a fact of some importance in view of the gradual depletion of iron ore reserves in the United States. The difficulty here is that the ores discovered to date are low-grade, too expensive to mine until large amounts of low-cost electric power are made available.

Alaska has a surfeit of potential power in its rivers and mountains, but very little of it is being exploited. The United States Reclamation Service states that Alaska is the largest undeveloped locale of hydroelectric energy in the world. Several major projects have been discussed for years without advancing beyond the talking stage. The Aluminum Company of America has been interested since 1952 in a $400,000,000 power development near Skagway to harness the headwaters of the Yukon River. But agreement was never forthcoming from Canada in whose area the Yukon rises.

The Harvey Aluminum Company, after three years of considera-
tion, dropped a project of similar size on the Copper River.

The biggest project of all has been proposed at the Ramparts, a
hundred miles northeast of Fairbanks. Here the Yukon is confined
between 300-foot walls of granite. A dam at this point would
probably create more power than Grand Coulee. It would provide
all the power needs of Alaska's vast interior. It would also form a
lake 150 miles long and 50 miles wide. University of Alaska
scientists say this lake would add several frost-free days to the
growing season and make Alaska's interior as productive an agricultural area as the North Central states. But a project of this
magnitude would require government financing as at Shasta, Grand
Coulee, and Boulder. It may well be that the first major efforts to
harness Alaska's streams and waterfalls will have to come not from
private industry but from the federal government.

One of Alaska's resources that is at last being used is its timber.
The visitor is struck by the great stands of virgin spruce and hemlock, particularly in southeast Alaska. Although conservation of
this resource is important in view of the reckless depletion earlier
in the century in the forests of the Pacific Northwest, countless
acres of Alaska timber have just been allowed to rot. Further-
more, government restrictions on lumber operations in the big
national forests have in the past kept down use of Alaska timber.
So has the fear of competition from Alaska by the Northwest
lumber interests. This resulted in some of the prohibitions on the
use and export of Alaska timber.

But Alaska timber has turned out to be ideally suited for pulp.
Government restrictions have been eased, and great multi-million
dollar industrial complexes have been rising in the forests of southeast Alaska. Ketchikan, Alaska's easternmost city and long its
salmon-fishing capital, is now the site of a $54,000,000 pulp mill
which has given employment to hundreds of workers and brought
something of a boom to the area. Sitka has been humming for the
last couple of years as the result of the $58,000,000 pulp mill being
erected there by Japanese industrialists. The city will, among other
things, have use of a new hydroelectric plant paid for in part by the
pulp mill which will get industrial water delivered directly from the

Pulp Mill at Ketchikan

tail-race. Big pulp mills are also being planned for Juneau and Wrangell.

Along with the prospectors hunting for Alaska's natural resources by plane have also come other prospectors. Shortly after statehood was announced, a group of seventy New York investment bankers made arrangements to tour Alaska by chartered plane in the spring of 1959 in order to look over the situation. There have been delegations of such new-style prospectors, from New York, Chicago, Washington state, Minneapolis, Japan, several northern European countries—and even from Texas. Bill Daniels, brother of Texas Governor Price Daniel, stepped off a plane in Nome and said, "You've got the know-how, we've got the capital and we want to help the big state of Alaska."

Logging operations at Ketchikan Pulp Mill

Almost any banker in Alaska will tell you that he has received numerous inquiries from potential investors all over the United States. Alaska needs the new capital badly. While several billion dollars in natural wealth has been taken out of Alaska, the total on deposit in Alaska banks in 1957 was about $160,000,000. The same Alaska businessmen who thump on the table in anger when they talk about "absentee owners" will tell you enthusiastically about the new prospectors in search of investment opportunities. It is hard to refrain from asking them the provocative question whether they aren't trying to get hold of new absentee capital at the very time that they are complaining about the activities of absentee owners.

"We want outside capital," is the almost invariable answer. "But we don't want monopolies that are able to take out without putting

back in and that can dominate our economy from Washington."
Back in 1907 a similar answer was given by the Valdez Prospect,
a critic of the Guggenheim-Morgan Alaska Syndicate, when it said
Alaska wanted "no handicap to corporate activity" except when it
became "political dictation by a handful of corporate interests."

The salmon-canning industry's lobby against statehood is a case
in point. So are the Syndicate's hit-and-run copper-mining operations which were a rich source of profit for a quarter of a century
but were abruptly terminated when no longer lucrative. There was
no effort to develop other Alaska sources of copper. The Syndicate's railroad was abandoned. Once-flourishing communities became ghost towns.

Statehood should make it possible to get outside capital on a
competitive basis so that no single group will be in a position to
dominate Alaska's politics and economics. Monopoly control in
Alaska is probably a thing of the past. One of the curious by-prod-
ucts of the new Klondike is the competition for Alaska business
between Portland and Seattle. For many years Seattle business interests enjoyed a virtual monopoly in Alaska. They controlled
Alaska's trade and commerce and transportation as well as its
salmon-canning industry. They preferred to keep things the way
they were. The Seattle Chamber of Commerce was the only one in
the country of any importance which refused to endorse statehood.
Now Portland, only 200 miles farther from Alaska, is trying to
cash in on the resentment of Alaska against Seattle.

The first governor to visit Alaska after statehood was Oregon's
Robert D. Holmes. He reported on his return that "Alaskans are
chafing under the trade monopoly of Seattle." When Miss Elinor
Moses of Fairbanks, a full-blooded Athabascan Indian, passed
through Portland en route to the Miss Universe contest in Long
Beach, California, she was wined and dined by the Portland
Chamber of Commerce. She didn't become Miss Universe, but she
liked Portland. Seattle businessmen in turn are trying to soothe the
bad feelings of past years.

It will take years for the new Klondike to reach its peak, before
Alaska is a fully industrialized state realizing the potential of its
resources. It will take time because there is still so much to be done.

Big houses being built in Alaska

Alaska needs improved transportation. It must bring living costs down, which in turn depends on transportation. The development of oil and mineral resources will help, since ships with consumer goods for Alaska will be able to haul back raw materials, thus reducing freight rates. Alaska needs a more developed agriculture, and it needs a food-processing industry which will reduce its dependence on imports. It needs a light manufacturing industry. It needs, above all, not a sudden and transitory gold rush, but an orderly development of its resources which will avoid the violent ups and downs of the past years. If this kind of development takes place, Alaska can be a Klondike for generations to come.

8: The Word Is Opportunity

A young agricultural expert shows the visitor around the Matanuska Valley. He drives to a farm where a gang of men is putting potatoes in bags, piling them up on a flat truck. On the way over he stops at a creek to look for a few minutes at the salmon spawning, writhing on little beds of gravel shortly before they die. He points to the craggy mountains rising out of the valley. "This is where we go hunting for mountain sheep," he says.

The young man, only 27, has an important job with the Alaska Department of Agriculture. A native of Idaho, he is a trained agronomist. Now he is tackling half a dozen important problems, helping farmers test the right crops in the new rich soil and find markets for their products.

"Why did you come to Alaska?" He looks a little surprised at the question. "Where else could I have an opportunity like this at my age, a good job, good pay, interesting work?"

A 40-year-old airline executive is describing the operations of his company. Locally financed, it has grown rapidly and carved out a stable business in southeast Alaska; it is the only means of transportation for many villages and even sizable towns. He saw Alaska for the first time when he was a Navy pilot, returned after the war to settle. "Where else," he asks, "could I be a top official of an airline at 40?"

The land has to be cleared

A vigorous man of 55, engaged in promoting the tourist business, is confronted with the same question. He is a busy man bursting with a dozen ideas, rushing from a Chamber of Commerce luncheon to meet a group of important financiers coming in at the airport from the States. His answer is couched in almost identical terms: "Where else could I have the opportunity to be a pioneer and build a new empire at 55?"

The word is opportunity. This is the magnet which has drawn thousands of men and women to Alaska since World War II and will draw thousands more. They are of different ages and different temperaments and have different interests. But almost invariably the common denominator is the opportunity to do big things, new things which they could not do back home.

Most of Alaska's food is still imported

It is in this sense that Alaska remains the last frontier. It is a frontier not only because much of it is still wild and unpopulated, and because conditions of life are still often rugged, but even more because it offers the challenge and the rewards of a new country. The word challenge is used by Alaskans almost as much as opportunity.

Inevitably Alaska attracts men and women who like to face up to a challenge. It draws pioneer types, people with daring and enterprise and new ideas. "If I hire a new employee," says a city official in Anchorage, "I want someone with a little romance in his soul." He probably means it. These are some of the qualities it is important to have in Alaska because there are frustrations and difficulties and hardships for new settlers in Alaska as well as opportunities. This, of course, is the meaning of challenge.

Farmers in Alaska have to clear the ground. Workers encounter the problem of seasonal employment. Business people have to face up to the problems of experimenting in new and uncertain fields. They can't always be sure a new idea will catch on. But given the knowledge that things won't necessarily come easily and a backlog of some cash against unemployment or temporary business reverses, Alaska still remains the greatest land of opportunity within the territorial limits of the United States.

Alaska is full of success stories. But it should be pointed out— as a qualifying remark—that they attract more attention than the saga of those who didn't quite make it during some of the difficult times of the past.

A rather daring one-legged man in Anchorage went skiing and broke his artificial leg. A short time later, he fell and broke his good leg. Laid up in bed with plenty of spare time on his hands, he got the idea of making his own artificial limb. Then he started making them for others. Now he has a flourishing little factory in the heart of town.

Charles B. West also got a hunch shortly after he settled down in Alaska. He had seen it for the first time during World War II as a commercial pilot. After the war he worked for a while as a bush pilot out of Fairbanks. Then he set up his own business which he called a bit grandiosely the Arctic Alaska Travel Service. His idea was to promote tourist travel to Alaska's Arctic areas, to Nome and to Eskimo villages like Kotzebue. The first winter in his $40-a-month office in Fairbanks was pretty lonesome. But soon the idea caught on. He branched out, organized plane tours, bus tours, chartered steamships. Within ten years he built up a $1,000,000 business.

John J. Teal, Jr., an expert on Arctic wild life, has a visionary idea that is yet to be tested in practice. But it is attracting the most serious attention throughout Alaska. He is trying to build up a new industry on the basis of the almost extinct musk-ox, one of the world's oldest domesticated animals. Teal says that the fleece of

Kodiak boat harbor

the musk-ox, known as quivit, is softer than cashmere and that textile manufacturers believe it can be used for fine clothing. The musk-ox used to roam the interior in considerable numbers. But they were killed off by hunters and are now so rare that Teal has been offered as much as $30,000 for one by a zoo. Teal is establishing an experimental breeding farm at the University of Alaska. There he will also study the problems of distributing musk-ox to ranchers for commercial use. A number of hard-headed business-men believe that musk-ox ranching can become an important in-dustry in Alaska's interior.

Government officials and successful businessmen in Alaska are convinced there is a rich field for small business in the new state. They suggest that new businessmen will have a better chance for success if they attempt to fill genuine needs and if they take ad-vantage of Alaska's resources and unique features. They also strongly emphasize the importance of some cash to start with.

Scrubbing a four-foot king crab

Alaska's interior is full of birch forests. You can see miles and miles of fine, straight birch trees driving along the Glenn Highway out of Anchorage. But nobody has done much about them. A few small furniture factories have started recently, and it is believed by many that there are good prospects in this field.

There are many possibilities in small-scale manufacturing, utilizing locally available resources and taking advantage of the fact that virtually all of Alaska's needs are now provided from outside. A chemist in Anchorage made a good thing out of collecting bone and suet which used to be shipped out for processing; he produced bone meal for the local market. Locally made bleaches and starches have begun appearing on grocery shelves around Anchorage. Potato

Tourist photographs a thawing lake

chips made out of Matanuska Valley potatoes can now be bought in the stores. But very little has been done to date to process vegetable and food products from the farms of the Matanuska and Tanana Valleys. Packaged frozen foods are almost all brought in and sold at high prices, despite the fact that plenty of local vegetables are available for freezing.

While the field has been pre-empted in salmon fishing and canning, there are openings for small business in the fish industry. There is room for shrimp fisheries in southeast Alaska, and for spider crab fishing in Nome. An oyster industry is considered feasible by the Bureau of Fisheries. But probably the best opportunities in connection with fish products are at the processing end. Smoked salmon is considered a good prospect; so are pickled salmon and herring and smoked sablefish. Cod, red snapper, rock cod, sole,

Fertile farm land in the Matanuska Valley

flounder and other bottom fish have been listed as offering possibilities for packaged quick-freeze food. Fur-trapping is as
crowded a field as fishing. But fur-ranching is a possibility which
has attracted many in Alaska. Most fur ranches have, however,
been unsuccessful due to poor markets, high costs, and animal
disease.

Perhaps the most immediate opportunities exist in connection
with what, surprisingly enough, is likely to become Alaska's biggest
industry, at least in the short run. This is tourism. Al Anderson, director of the Alaska Resource Development Board, lists it
ahead of petroleum and minerals in outlining immediate growth
possibilities. In fact, tourism, now attracting about $30,000,000 a

A farm near Palmer

year in business to Alaska, is already the second biggest industry there. Alaskans believe that within the next few years it can be built up to $100,000,000 a year. While some of the big projects for building up Alaska tourism involve considerable outlays of capital, there are many other modest ways to meet the needs of the growing tourist trade.

Visitors to Alaska will be struck by the fact that it has few good restaurants—and very few indeed that do anything with local Alaska foods. Only occasionally does one run across a restaurant which features king crab, salmon, shrimp, or moose and caribou steaks and chops. Good small restaurants with a little flair and atmosphere would attract not only the tourist trade, they could also cater to Alaskans the year around. While there are a number of

Harvesting in the Matanuska Valley

good motels and lodges on Alaska's highways, there will be need for more. Four young men have been building an all-year ski resort near Fairbanks, and there are undoubtedly many possibilities for vacation, hunting, fishing and sports facilities of all kinds.

Alaska has about three million acres of potential farm land, land for raising vegetables, growing grains, raising beef cattle and poultry, and establishing dairy farms. But less than one percent of this potential, only about 20,000 acres, is now under cultivation. Much of the farm land in Alaska is excellent, and the visitor will be impressed by the rich, dark soil. Since Alaska now imports most of its food, the long-range demand for farm products will be high and the outlook for agriculture good.

There are now about 500 farms in Alaska, some of them mod-

A housing project in Fairbanks

ern, well equipped and comparing with their counterparts in the other forty-eight states. Some farmers net as much as $10,000 a year, but the average runs closer to $4,000. Dairying accounts for about half the commercial production of Alaska farms; potatoes run second and poultry products—despite the high cost of importing feed—third. What many farmers have done during their starting period is to work part-time while getting the land cleared and ready for production. This is a sensible approach for farmers settling in Alaska.

But the Alaska Department of Agriculture and other farm agencies strongly advise would-be settlers to take a trip to Alaska first in order to size up the situation before bringing their families. There are excellent reasons for this. While farmers can get home-

Anchorage—old and new

steads without buying their land, the cost of clearing the trees and
brush is very high, ranging between $100 and $250 an acre. Costs
for feed and farm equipment—most of it imported—also run high.
Markets are still limited—largely because stores in the cities tend to
adhere to their pattern of buying from Seattle. As Alaska develops,
the home market will increase. Costs will come down, and roads
and other facilities will improve the prospects for farming. This is
unquestionably one of the areas of opportunity in Alaska. It is not,
however, a way to get rich quick; nor is it something to plunge into
without careful and realistic exploration.

Government land is also available for other purposes. It may be
obtained for homesites for $2.50 an acre, and larger tracts can be
purchased from the government at low prices for industrial sites.
Builders and project developers have done well in Anchorage and
Fairbanks. Some amateurs have bought real estate, developed it,
and sold it at a substantial profit. It would be unwise, however, to
invest on the hunch that big fortunes can be made in real estate
speculation. Much of the choice land around the larger cities has

A new home in Anchorage

already been bought or is tied up in military reservations. Privately owned land in Alaska cities commands surprisingly high prices.

The job picture in Alaska has been uneven. The big military constructions projects brought in thousands of workers from the states, many of whom stayed in Alaska. As the projects were completed, there was unemployment in Anchorage and other cities. The Alaska Employment Service warns that construction workers would be unwise to come to Alaska unless they have definite jobs provided by contractors or through unions. But there are a number of other occupations in which there is a demand for personnel. The greatest need is for specialized skills rather than for general labor.

Government is one of the big industries in Alaska, and there is a constant need for stenographers and secretaries. Surprising numbers of young women come to Alaska from all over the United States to work in government offices. They are drawn partly by higher wages, 25 percent higher than for comparable civil service jobs elsewhere in the United States. This is offset, however, by the greater cost of living, which varies from region to region but which is at least 25 percent higher. The biggest lure is probably Alaska's two-to-one proportion of men to women.

Engineers of all kinds are in demand. So are geologists and mining experts. Electronic and radio technicians can get jobs with-

Skilled workers overhauling an airplane engine

out difficulty. Young graduates of professional schools can find real opportunities in Alaska. There is particular need for dentists and for medical specialists of all kinds.

Teaching is one of the professions which will find a fertile field in Alaska for a long time to come. Alaska schools are generally good,

More teachers are needed for the expanding school system

and qualifications for teachers are about the same as those required in the United States. But wages run higher. Minimum salaries required by law range between $4,500 and $7,600. Schools have the option of increasing the starting wage—and often do pay between $500 and $1,000 more.

A teacher's life in Anchorage or Fairbanks or Juneau is not altogether out of line with his or her experience. Venturesome teachers, in search of something challenging and especially rewarding, find jobs in the schools maintained by the Bureau of Indian Affairs in small native communities. Here a spirit of adventure and real dedication is essential. Instructions to teachers newly arrived at a native village include this advice: "Oil stoves need to be kept clean. . . . Check the stove pipes and chimney and be sure they are clean. If not, clean or replace them on the spot. If you are one of those gifted people for whom inanimate things work with joy, you are indeed blessed. If you must struggle to bring an ornery stove to heel, set your teeth and grimly plod onward. The stove was made by human hands, and you've come this far under your own power, so likely perseverance will win this day as many another!"

The new teacher is told in the same manual to count on the bush pilot for moral support and countless favors: "If you gripe about your assignment, manufacture difficulties where none exist and broadcast your case of cabin-fever as having had no equal in history, don't be surprised if you find yourself up Muck Creek without a paddle. Be a good sport and everyone will rally to support you, the bush pilot first of all."

"The foundation of Christian civilization," the teacher is instructed, "is a respectful approach to another individual. . . . The native peoples of Alaska deserve your respect. They have made a radical adjustment in their living habits that permits them to flourish under conditions of the most adverse nature."

Teachers in isolated villages may often do other chores for the Bureau of Indian Affairs or the Territorial Department of Public Welfare. They may give first aid in emergencies, serve as radio-telephone operators, or help run the native co-operative store. In view of the multiplicity of duties, husband and wife teams are given preference. In some larger villages there is room for both to teach. In other cases, the husband or wife of the teacher is usually employed as an assistant at about two thirds of the salary. Despite the obviously arduous duties and the far from munificent salaries, many devoted young people are drawn to the native schools as teachers. Here is not much money but plenty of challenge and opportunity.

Alaska's greatest need is for people with enterprise and education. Government officials also add that a backlog of cash is necessary. In their enthusiasm most businessmen tend to minimize this factor. "I don't give a damn if people don't have a dime," says a Nome banker. "There is opportunity for youth here. We need to triple our population." A Fairbanks businessman says, "There is opportunity for youth here. He doesn't have to have money. He does have to have initiative." The manual for native school teachers contains this bit of philosophy, "There is some speculation among older residents that the Stateside people learn more in Alaska than they teach!" To this might be added the thought that those who put their energy and brains to work in building Alaska will probably receive more than they give.

9: Life with Zest

Antonio Polet came to Nome in 1900, an Italian immigrant boy. While others prospected or panned gold on the beaches in the boom city of those days, he became a peddler. It was a lowly business, but one that paid off. Soon he was a prosperous merchant and a leading citizen. The store he founded, Polet's, no longer deals in general merchandise, but it is a successful gift shop with a fine collection of native handicrafts. His daughter, Mrs. Emily Boucher, now carries on the family business. She runs back and forth between Polet's and the thrice-weekly *Nome Nugget* a few doors away which she publishes. "The farthest north Associated Press paper in the world," Mrs. Boucher says.

"Now we are raising three third-generation Alaskans," she says. "They like Alaska just as we do. I wouldn't want to live anywhere else, and they wouldn't either. One of my sons went to the University of Virginia for two years. He liked it all right. It was a good school. But he decided to finish his education at the University of Alaska."

Waino E. Hendrickson, Alaska's last acting governor before statehood, tells a similar story. His father came to Alaska at the turn of the century. Waino was born in Juneau and went to the public school there. Of the 14 students in his graduating class, nine are still in Juneau and five have grandchildren in Juneau schools.

Squatter's hut on the Yukon River

All this is not intended to suggest that Alaska has had a stable population for the last three generations. It has not. There are still thousands of workers who come in from the states for the spring and summer, cannery workers and some construction workers. But this is a constantly diminishing group. Alaska now has a labor force adequate for most purposes. There are less part-time Alaskans than ever before. While tens of thousands of the pioneers who flocked into Alaska during the gold rush left after their dreams of wealth petered out, a significant number remained. There is an even larger number who came in the last 15 years, young men who first saw Alaska while they were in the armed forces and then returned after the war. "An Alaskan by choice" was Senator Gruening's successful slogan in the November 1958 election. There

Alaskans looking at a glacier

are now thousands and thousands of people who consider themselves Alaskans—whether by birth or choice or both.

They give different reasons for preferring Alaska. A young man in Juneau sounds like a page out of an old Rex Beach or Jack London novel. "You can trust people here," he says. "Nobody will double-cross you. If a man gives you his word in a business deal, he will keep it." Another, who lives 10 miles out of Juneau and drives in to work in his Volkswagen, prefers it because "you have elbow room here, you aren't crowded." He is a bit nervous though that too many people will flock in with statehood. "People are friendlier here," others will tell you. "They will help you if you are in trouble." Many emphasize the outdoor life, the hunting and fishing available close to all the sizable population centers, and

Alaskans on an outing at Camp Denali near McKinley Park

the wild beauty of Alaska's scenery. Most persons, however, stress opportunity as their primary motive for living in Alaska, although they often mention other factors too.

Alaskans are people of all kinds in appearance, attitude, temperament. You wouldn't be able to spot them if you saw them anywhere else in the United States. But they are as distinctive in their own way as Texans or New Englanders. There is an unashamed feeling of patriotism and love of country among Alaskans which might sound a little inflated and old-fashioned if you heard it elsewhere. "I love Alaska," bursts out a Fairbanks businessman who is talking quietly in his modern living room about the economic prospects in the area. "My whole heart is tied up in this country."

Anchorage

People generally tend to dress more informally than in most other places in the United States. You will see businessmen and officials in their traditional business-suit uniform. But you will also see them in their offices wearing sport shirts and bolo ties with a gleaming stone on a black string. Eccentricity in dress or manner is ignored. Beards are more common than elsewhere, except perhaps in our college towns. A hotel owner in Nome, always garbed in a flannel shirt, sports a long mustache curving up to two finely groomed tips and constantly has a dachshund on a leash. Nobody pays any attention.

The informality goes beyond externals. It is easy to walk in on anybody in Alaska from the governor down. You find fewer stuffed shirts in high places. Government officials are blunter, franker,

Dogs getting set to race in Anchorage

more outspoken. They tell you the bad along with the good. Businessmen are "boosters" all right. But they don't try to fool you or gloss over problems when they talk to you. People speak more freely. The words "off the record" are rarely, if ever, heard.

There is a drive and a push and an excitement among Alaskans which is perhaps the most distinctive characteristic of Alaska living. Everybody you talk to is bursting with some plan or scheme, an idea for a ferry system to connect southeast Alaska with the Alaska highway or for a new business that might be started up or for a new crop that might grow in the Matanuska Valley. There is a feeling of purpose and hope. Alaskans don't believe their state will remain the same. They expect Alaska to grow, and they expect to grow along with it. They are among the last of American individualists, the kind you used to find in frontier country.

The same individualism prevails in politics. While Alaska tends to vote Democratic, the outcome of elections is never certain. The legislature has gone overwhelmingly Republican in one election, just as decisively Democratic in the next. "It's the individual that counts, not the party," Alaskans explain.

At the same time, Alaskan individualists are also strong on co-operation, probably the same kind of co-operation forced on pioneers everywhere. You can find this on almost any level. People do help each other. Drive along the road and get a flat tire or get stuck on a soft shoulder, and the next car that passes will stop automatically. In fact, two or three cars may stop just to make sure you are all right. Paradoxically, individualistic Alaskans are great joiners. Almost everybody belongs to some organization. The first Yukon pioneers started to form organizations even before the Klondike strike, and their successors have kept on joining. There are dozens of lodges, clubs, fraternal orders, service organizations.

Individualistic Alaskans take for granted a substantial role for government in developing their economy. Power plants and other public utilities are publicly owned in Fairbanks, Anchorage, and most other Alaska cities. The Alaska Railroad is owned by the United States Government and operated by the Department of Interior. Several private corporations had started railroads and failed or else built railroads that served only specific industries for a limited time. The federal government has helped finance co-operatively owned stores in native villages and several co-operative canneries. It also started in 1935 Alaska's largest agricultural community, the Matanuska Valley colony.

For a long time it was no secret that this valley had wonderful soil for farming. Back in 1900, George Palmer, who had a trading post in this area, planted a little garden and reported, "Parsnips are the finest and largest I ever saw. . . . Turnips grow to an enormous size, and of fine flavor. . . . Rutabagas are large and fine. . . . Lettuce, peas, radishes, cauliflower, and potatoes are a success." Hardy homesteaders settled from time to time in the rich valley. But they were up against the difficulties of clearing the

A 43-pound cabbage grown at Matanuska Valley

land of virgin forests and heavy underbrush, of rugged winter weather, of getting their produce to market without adequate roads. It took a major government project during the depression years to put farming in the Matanuska Valley on a firm basis, and then it took the voluntary co-operation of the farmers to make a success of their colony.

Today the Matanuska Valley is a prosperous farming community. The farmers really grow out-size cabbages there, 40 pounds or more a head. In fact, they will tell you privately that those big cabbages, grown for display and promotion purposes, are something of a nuisance; they are too big for marketing. So they grow cabbages closer together than in most places in order to get the heads down to a convenient size. You visit attractive modern homes on some of the farms. The homes have electricity, good television reception, telephone service; color phones are in great demand. The trading center is called Palmer; it is a bustling town

Cabbage grown at Arctic Circle Hot Springs, in the far north

with a population of about 2,000, with a modern high school, an up-to-date grade school, a public library, a department store, a hotel and restaurants.

The center of life in this prosperous area is the Matanuska Valley Farmers Co-operating Association, a $5,500,000 organization. Most of the valley's 250 farm families are members of the producer-consumer co-op. A modern co-op dairy produces Matanuska Maid milk and ice cream. Co-op warehouses store home-grown carrots and lettuce and potatoes. A big co-op feed mill is expected to furnish feed to the farmers at lower prices; the co-op's Trading Post does a flourishing retail business, supplies groceries, hardware and farm implements at prices well below those asked in other markets.

The electricity is furnished by a co-operative; so is the telephone service. When you pick up the local telephone book, you get an echo of the hardship and trouble and the joint effort it took to build up this successful agricultural community. The directory begins with a "Brief History of the Matanuska Telephone Association, Inc." which states, "The struggle for a practical valley-wide telephone system started in the very early colony days when the Alaska Rural Rehabilitation Corporation strung the first telephone lines to serve the construction camps and a saw mill. . . ." The "struggle" continued for a long time; telephone service didn't become a reality until 1955.

Farm life in Alaska is now far from the lonely existence you might expect. While there are some farm homesteaders in isolated areas on the Kenai Peninsula, most Alaska farmers are either in the Matanuska Valley, near Palmer and only about 40 miles from Anchorage, or in the Tanana Valley which is near Fairbanks. They spend long weekends hunting and fishing. They fill their freezers with moose meat and salmon. But they also have most of the city conveniences, and they can readily drive into the city to visit with friends or see a movie.

Unions are taken for granted in Alaska as much as Chambers of Commerce and co-operatives. In fact, union buttons are as much in evidence in Alaska towns as on the streets of San Francisco. There is hardly a restaurant or a construction project or a cannery in Alaska that is staffed by non-union labor. There is no serious challenge to organized labor as an important part of Alaska economic and even political life. Alaska has an advanced program of social and labor legislation, and the kind of "right-to-work" legislation passed in some states finds little support there.

Fishing for rainbow trout

But there is a good deal of complaining about "absentee labor," a term of abuse used almost as often as "absentee capital" and referring to workers brought in from the outside for the canneries or for construction jobs. There is a feeling that some of these workers take away jobs from local labor, and that the unions to which the former belong are run from the outside. There are also frequent complaints about high wages, and some people argue that unions are responsible for the high cost of living. But most Alaskans, including business leaders, single out transportation costs as the principal reason for high prices.

R. E. McFarland, president of the Alaska Federation of Labor, listens courteously to complaints against the unions, but answers firmly. He believes that the "absentee labor" problem is rapidly becoming a thing of the past, except perhaps in the fish canneries. He says that about 90 percent of the construction labor is now local and that the affairs of Alaska labor are determined in Alaska rather than in Seattle or San Francisco.

McFarland answers grumblings about high wages with a series of questions. "Do you know what the scale for common labor is in San Francisco?" When the answer is slow in coming, he suggests that it is about $2.80 an hour. "Now do you know how much higher the cost of living is in Anchorage than in San Francisco? Well, it's about 43 percent. When you add that 43 percent to the basic pay rate and then realize that labor is so much more seasonal in Alaska than elsewhere, you'll begin to see that our $4-an-hour wage scale is not out of line." McFarland does add that as better transportation and a more developed economy bring living costs down, Alaska's labor will be ready to discuss an adjustment of pay scales. Where steady work has been forthcoming, as at the Ketchikan pulp mill, unions have been willing to tone down wage demands.

The cost of living is about 25 percent higher in southeast Alaska than in Seattle, about 50 percent higher in Fairbanks and the Interior. Even relatively inflexible government pay has been inflated to meet Alaska conditions. It is 25 percent higher than in the other forty-eight states. Women in Alaska work even more generally than elsewhere, which is also in part an attempt to overcome high prices.

The resulting standard of living is about the same as elsewhere in the United States, perhaps a bit higher. One quite typical couple in Fairbanks has a handsomely furnished apartment in one of the modern buildings where native children ride up and down the elevators for amusement; the kids know all about airplanes, but elevators are something new. The husband works as a skilled craftsman on one of the Air Force bases nearby; the wife is a government worker. They live up to their income, but they don't have any real trouble getting by and can afford eating out and occasional entertaining.

On the whole, Alaskans don't talk much about high prices. They take them in their stride. "I'd scream when I first came to Alaska," says a Fairbanks housewife, "about paying $1 for a small package

Northern Lights over Fairbanks

of hot dogs or 40 cents for a loaf of bread. But you get used to it because salaries are higher than in the states." There is very little comment on the high price of gasoline, which runs to about 50 cents a gallon for regular gasoline in the Fairbanks area. You see quite a few Volkswagens and other small foreign cars in Alaska. But drivers rarely mention economy as a factor. They feel that a small car is more convenient or point out that European air-cooled motors don't freeze in the winter.

Alaskans also pay less attention to the weather than you would expect. In southeast Alaska they are accustomed to the summer rains and to the fogs which often throw airplane travel off schedule. A number of Alaskans in Fairbanks and other cities will assure you that they actually look forward to winter. They don't seem to mind the cold which goes down to 40° below and even lower. For

U. S. Coast Guardsmen playing baseball in subzero sunshine on
shore-fast ice near Saint Lawrence Island

short walks or drives many of them don't bother with woolen under-
wear or parkas and mukluks. For longer exposure to the cold they
dress more adequately, of course, and their homes are kept very
warm. They say winter driving is not difficult. The snow gets
powdered fine, and there is no skidding or sliding. "It's like riding
over a fine layer of sand," says a taxi-driver. Of course, cars do
require extra attention. There are electric hitching posts in garages
and at the military bases where head-bolt heaters are attached
to the engine block. They are plugged in at least two or three hours
before the car is needed.

In most of Alaska the winter is the holiday season. The northern
lights give the winter skies a festive illumination. "We work harder

Two lady dog mushers after a race in Fairbanks

and longer during the long summer days," a Nome businessman says. "We get used to going for days and days almost without sleep. Then we heave a sigh of relief when winter comes. That's our social season. We take it easier. We have time to relax and to visit around." The Eskimos, too, follow this pattern of the seasons.

There are big winter festivals which Alaskans hope in time

Ski lift by helicopter

will compete with the New Orleans Mardi Gras and similar tourist attractions. The annual Anchorage Fur Rendezvous in February is a combination fur market and carnival. There are dog-team races, with entries from all over Alaska; an Eskimo seal-hunt pageant, complete with the butchering of real seals, is staged in the municipal auditorium. Fairbanks competes with the Alaska Ice Carnival in March. Here one can see a baseball game played on snowshoes. There is also an art exhibit and a curling bonspiel. Curling, a Scottish bowling game played on ice, is a popular winter sport. So are skiing, ice skating, and ice hockey. There is a good deal of bowling in the winter too.

One of the big events of the year in Alaska is the annual Nenana ice pool. The beginning of spring is dated from the start of the break-up of the ice on the Nenana River. Almost everybody in

The Douglas Ski Bowl near Juneau

Alaska buys tickets for betting on the exact time of the break-up. Up-to-date scientific methods and astrology have both failed to make the exact prediction.

There are also festivals of various kinds during the summer. Fairbanks has a Golden Days celebration to recall the old days of the gold rush; Skagway has a similar Days of '98 festival featuring the legends of the local bad man, Soapy Smith. There are salmon derbies in the southeast, and a big celebration in the Eskimo village of Kotzebue to mark the catching of the first whale. There are agricultural fairs in the Matanuska and Tanana Valleys.

But primarily summer is a time for work—and for outdoor sports. The summer is a busy season, and Alaskans work hard and play hard. There are boat races, baseball games, swimming, camping. Above all, there are fishing and hunting; the hunting season opens

Old cabins in Fairbanks contrast with home opposite

in August. After work many sportsmen fly their private planes out to a nearby lake for an evening of fishing during the long summer daylight. There are more private airplanes per capita in Alaska than anywhere else in the world.

These activities add a zest to city living in Alaska. There is also a civic-mindedness in Alaska's cities that seems to go beyond what you will find elsewhere. School bond issues are approved without difficulty. Urban renewal programs, designed at eliminating eyesores like the ramshackle Fairbanks log cabins near the modern apartment buildings, are pressed vigorously. Improvements, like paved streets, sewers, street lights, are constantly being made.

Alaskans show a concern with education which is quite remarkable. The newest and biggest public buildings are the schools. Sometimes the streets near the schools will still be unpaved, but the school buildings themselves will be as fine and modern as you will find anywhere.

A modern home in Fairbanks a block from old cabins

Almost everywhere in Alaska people will ask, "Have you seen our university yet?" Dr. Ernest Patty, the president of the University of Alaska, is mentioned more often and with greater praise than any elected official in Alaska. The university has an enrollment of about 750 students. Its academic standing is excellent. Strong points are geology, mining, and anthropology. Recently it has also been strengthening its humanities department. It offers several graduate degrees but does not yet have law and medical schools. The Geophysical Institute at the university has some of the world's finest facilities for studying the Arctic. Other features are fine collections of native art objects and of Alaska literature. There is no cost of living problem at the university. All expenses, including tuition and room and board, come to $465 a semester. The university also provides opportunities for study at community colleges it supervises at Anchorage, Juneau, and Ketchikan.

Alaska has a respect for education and for professors quite at

Fourth of July parade in Nome

variance with what is found in many more sophisticated urban centers in the United States, and certainly in sharp contrast to what you would expect to find in our last frontier. One reason for this is that Alaska urgently needs its university and its excellent school system. If it hopes to grow, it needs educated, trained youth. Alaskans point out that the university is one of the magnets keeping young people in Alaska and preventing the population drift prevalent in former years.

But there is also an interest in education which goes beyond the directly practical. Alaskans are as proud of the university's anthropology courses as of its mining curriculum. Respect for cul-

New high school in Anchorage

ture generally contrasts with some of the cruder aspects of Alaska life, such as the tough bars you will find in any Alaska city. But this deep-seated attitude toward culture is an aspect of Alaska life more significant in the long run than the external crudeness.

The visitor to Anchorage is likely to be told by a city dignitary or a leading businessman, "You must look in on our little theater movements." There are three little theaters in Anchorage, and the same number in Fairbanks. Recent productions have included Arthur Miller's *The Crucible* and Shaw's *Pygmalion*. The Alaska Music Trail, which sponsors leading artists in Alaska appearances, has been a spectacular success.

Anchorage boasts a fine public library with 25,000 volumes, Great Books clubs, and a chapter of the League of Western Writers. It has a 40-member Symphony Orchestra and a Community Chorus with 100 voices. There is considerable interest in painting and good photography. The Anchorage Film Society offers off-beat American and foreign films. Perhaps the most remarkable thing is that all this is looked on with the greatest public favor. Men will tell you that it offers women a cultural outlet and helps integrate them into Alaska life. But the men have also become unmistakably interested in the cultural activity in Anchorage.

Some of this is reminiscent of the attitudes prevalent in the Old West 50 or 75 years ago. There was hardly a frontier town which did not boast its opera house and its share of visiting operatic and theatrical stars. In Alaska, there is still some of that frontier pride in learning and art. It is one aspect of Alaska living which one hopes will not be destroyed as the new state grows and prospers.

10: All of Alaska

"What are the most popular tourist spots?" former Governor Mike Stepovich was asked in an interview with *United States News and World Report.*

"All of Alaska," he said. "Some like the southeastern part a little better than they do the Interior, and others like the Interior better than they do the southeast.

"All of Alaska is quite beautiful. In the southeastern part you have the glaciers, you have the high mountains. And in the Interior you have the wide-open spaces and the beautiful summers and the midnight sun. And then you have the little villages where the native people live. People go and watch their dances and the way they do things."

Even discounting the inevitable diplomacy of a politician wooing the voters, Stepovich was not far wrong. All of Alaska is worth seeing, and each part has its own particular appeal. Where you go depends on how you come to Alaska, on how much money you can spend, and on what you want to do and see.

Most people now come to Alaska by plane. It is quick and relatively inexpensive, 2½ hours from Seattle to Ketchikan, $49 one way. Once in Alaska, you get around by plane without wasting much time. As one writer puts it, all Alaska is "plane-happy." Plane travel in Alaska is quite informal, because local planes also

Pausing to look at a glacier

provide taxi, bus, and freight service for many areas. Free-lance bush pilots are ready to fly you anywhere, at any time; they have pioneered air travel in the region. Don't be surprised to see cartons of canned goods in the cabin, or even a hunter's moose or a cement mixer. And don't fret too much if you miss connections because your plane has to deliver a power generator to a native hospital or groceries to a local store. The use of airplanes for passenger and freight transport is a dramatic chapter in Alaska's present-day development.

Plane travel in Alaska can also be quite beautiful. Flying out of Fairbanks you often see Mount McKinley's snow-covered crown rising abruptly out of the flat plateau. You can see Glacier Bay

Seeing Alaska by auto

and the wild beautiful coast from Juneau to Anchorage, the wooded islands, the great forests between Juneau and Sitka. On the other hand, there is a lot you don't see from a plane, especially if it is cloudy. And while getting to Alaska by air is not expensive, the cost of traveling around by plane mounts up.

Auto travel is probably the best way to get the feel of the country, the closest view of the majestic scenery. It is still something of a rugged trip over the Alaska Highway, but thousands do it every year—preferably from mid-June to mid-September. It will get even more popular as the gravel stretches of highway in Canada

Valley of the 10,000 smokes, Katmai National Monument

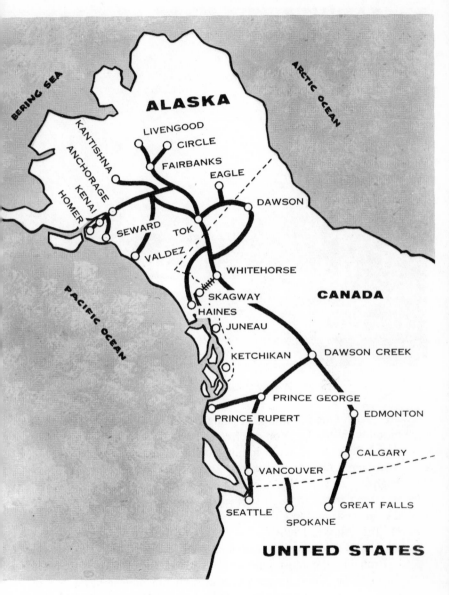

The Alaska Highway, and connecting roads

A view along the Haines cut-off

are paved. One advantage of going by car is that it gives you great mobility in Alaska. You are free to drive to Mount McKinley National Park, to visit old mining towns or remote Indian villages. You can really see the country, drive past glaciers on the Glenn Highway, or watch herds of buffalo grazing on the range. However, you can't travel through southeast Alaska by auto or to Nome in the far west; and to go from the United States border to Fairbanks on the Alaska Highway—a distance of 2,350 miles—requires about 6–8 days under normal conditions.

Probably the most enjoyable way to visit Alaska is by ship through the famed inside passage. You are almost never out of sight of land as your ship threads its way through a bewildering

A view on the Kenai Peninsula

maze of sweet-smelling, spruce-covered islands. You stop off at Skagway, Ketchikan, Juneau, or other southeast Alaska cities. This trip costs as little as $200 in the early June off-season. While a cruise is the way to see southeast Alaska, it won't, however, get you to the Interior.

All the main methods of travel have pluses and minuses. But it is also possible to make a number of combinations of auto and ship or ship and plane on your own, or to get variety by taking any one of a number of tours. These will usually take you through the inside passage by boat, then continue by plane, bus, railroad, or all three. Comprehensive tours of about 20 days cost $500 and up. (For more detailed information on tours, see the Supplement.)

(Top) A tourist boat going through the Inside Passage, and
(bottom) tourists on a Passage cruise boat

Endicott Arm in the Inside Passage

Aerial view of Ketchikan, with fishing fleet in the foreground
and the Tongass National Forest in the background

Going by ship or plane, you will probably stop at Ketchikan
first, a town of about 7,000 clinging to the side of Deer Mountain.
Ketchikan was a supply center for miners in the 1890's and then
became Alaska's great salmon-fishing and packing center which it
still is. It has also become a center for Alaska's growing pulp
industry. Only two miles away is Saxman Park, site of many old
totem poles, and 11 miles away is Mud Bight where you can see a
native ceremonial house and other historic totem poles. Mountains,
waterways, and waterfalls surround the town which is on an island.
It is fine salmon- and steelhead-fishing country.

The first thing you are likely to see when you get to Juneau is

Juneau, the capital, with old gold mine at the right

the red-roofed buildings of the abandoned Alaska-Juneau Gold Mine, the Juneau Glory Hole it used to be called. Then look up and you will see two massive mountains, Mount Roberts and Mount Juneau, which dominate Alaska's capital city. Juneau somehow combines the atmosphere of an old frontier town and of a staid, settled community. Wooden canopies extend out to the street from some store fronts, providing both a whiff of the old days and protection against the rain. Across the narrow Gastineau Channel from Juneau is the old Treadwell mine on Douglas Island, also abandoned.

There is no longer any gold mining in the area. But fishing, lumbering, and government are now the principal industries, partic-

The Mendenhall Glacier viewed from a log chapel at Auk Lake

ularly the latter. From Juneau it is a short auto or bus ride to the
spectacular Mendenhall Glacier and a short plane or boat trip to
Glacier Bay National Monument, where you can see about 20
glaciers flowing from an ice-cap high among 15,000-foot mountains.
Great chunks of ice break off the glaciers and float in the bay. From
Juneau you can also visit Indian fishing villages like Hoonah and
Angoon.

Sitka is not on the main travel routes, but this town of 4,000
on Baranof Island is worth the trouble of a special trip if only
for its beauty. There is something breath-taking about Sitka, as
you land by amphibian plane on the water, then taxi to dry land,
and look around at the snow-covered mountain and the islands deep
green with spruce and the blue passageways and inlets of the ocean
and the fishing boats nestling in the harbor. But Sitka is also well
worth seeing for a dozen other reasons. It is a principal meeting-

Sitka from the air

ground of old and new in Alaska. This is the old Russian capital, and you can see the relics of the past in St. Michael's Cathedral or in the little Russian graveyard. Here you will see beautiful totem poles in the Sitka National Monument, a short walk from the center of town, and the ultra-modern $58,000,000 new pulp mill built with Japanese capital. Here is a fine museum with Indian handicrafts at the Sheldon Jackson School, and across a narrow channel is the Mt. Edgecumbe High School operated by the Bureau of Indian Affairs. If you have the time, stop off and chat with some of the wonderful old-timers at the Pioneers' Home. There are real veterans of the Yukon gold rush here, and they can give you a feeling of the lure of gold and of the hardships and heart-breaks of the Klondike days you are not likely to get elsewhere.

(Top) The Chief Shakes Community House at Wrangell, and
(bottom) remains of old Indian community house in Southeast Alaska

Lake Spenard, Anchorage

There are also smaller towns in southeast Alaska you shouldn't miss. Skagway, on the steamship routes and tours, retains much of the flavor of the gold rush days when it was a major supply center and jumping-off place for the Yukon. Here are false-front buildings, and the grave of Soapy Smith, Skagway's most celebrated citizen as well as its most notorious. In Wrangell you will see the Chief Shakes Community House, one of those common dwelling places for a group of families which so shocked the early missionaries; it now houses a fine collection of utensils and art objects. Petersburg, a shrimp-fishing center, is a bit of old Scandinavia in Alaska. The lawns are well kept, the houses gay. There are some floating houses on rafts in the harbor, and these are also immaculately neat with bright-red paint and window curtains.

A view of Mount McKinley from the Alaska Railroad

You get to Anchorage by plane—a direct flight from Seattle—and you can drive down from Fairbanks if you reach Alaska by car. The 1939 WPA *Guide to Alaska* describes it as a small railroad town with a population of 2,277. Now, twenty years later, there are 60,000 people in the Anchorage area, about 90,000 if you include the military at nearby bases. Anchorage was founded as junction of the Alaska Railroad. But now it is the center of the new in Alaska, of the recent oil and mining developments which are changing the face of the forty-ninth state. If an oil boom comes to Alaska, it is Anchorage which will be the metropolis of the new industry. From Anchorage prospectors fly to look for new oil fields and new deposits of scarce minerals.

Anchorage—a modern, bustling city

Anchorage isn't particularly picturesque. It is just raw and new and exciting, with its suburban housing developments, wide streets, lively business district, three radio stations, two TV stations, two daily newspapers, and all its plans for growth and expansion. Anchorage is one of the few places in Alaska where you get some feeling of the wealth that is beginning to flow to Alaskans. You see suburbs with $100,000 homes and a landing field for private planes.

From Anchorage it is a short trip by bus or auto to the Matanuska Valley, Alaska's agricultural center. Anchorage is the vantage point

Seward—the flavor of old Alaska

from which to see the spectacular Kenai Peninsula with its great
moose range and rugged mountains, and Seward, an old port and
fishing town and starting point of the Alaska Railroad, which
has not shared in the recent economic boom and has more of the
old-time Alaska flavor than its bigger rival.

Many people believe you haven't really been in Alaska until
you've seen Fairbanks and the Interior. Fairbanks, even more than
Sitka, combines dramatically aspects of Alaska's past and its future.
Here are still standing the decrepit log cabins of old prospectors

The old red-light district in Fairbanks, now a run-down business area to be torn down in their urban renewal program

and old settlers, and here are ultra-modern apartment buildings and a fever of planning to renovate the city and all Alaska. Fairbanks is still something of a rude frontier town—at the same time that it boasts Alaska's fine and growing university. It is a rapidly changing city with its population of 15,000 and about 35,000 in the area. It has a modern hospital, three banks, a golf and country club, two radio stations, two TV stations, a plush motel—and too many bars to count.

Fairbanks is in the heart of the old gold-mining country, the land of trappers and hunters. From Fairbanks there are tourist side-trips by bus or auto or plane or even river boat. You can make arrangements to visit old mining and trading towns like Circle and Fort Yukon, now Indian villages where the women still do their intricate bead work on moose hide and where the people still

Indian Fish Trap on the Yukon River near Fort Yukon

live by hunting and fishing. Occasional Indian fishing wheels are still seen on the edge of rivers. At Fort Yukon, where the summer heat is almost as extreme as the 70°-below winter cold, luscious strawberries and 10-foot sunflowers grow big under the midnight sun.

Although some Arctic tours now take in Nome, it stands isolated on the Bering Sea from the rest of Alaska except by plane and is missed by many visitors. Nome, with a population of only about 2,000 left, has not shared in Alaska's postwar economic boom. The streets are unpaved, many of the houses decrepit or deserted or both. There is much unemployment. Nome has deteriorated badly since the years when thousands of eager prospectors tramped its streets. Repeatedly it has been devastated by fire and storm.

"But Nome doesn't die," says a local merchant. Somehow it has survived everything, and somehow it still exudes perhaps more

(Top) Swimming Pool at Circle Hot Springs, just inside the Arctic Circle, and (bottom) children around post office at Fort Yukon

Muir Lake and Mount McKinley in McKinley National Park

than any other town in Alaska the feeling of the old days as you
wander past its seven bars and seven churches. In the bars you
can see old photos and pages of newspapers of a bygone era head-
lining each new discovery of gold. You can visit Rex Beach's old
cabin, walk on the beaches once crowded with men panning gold.
Nome is full of sad reminders of the heroic past and of a gallant con-
viction among its residents that one way or another it still faces
a heroic future when mining revives or when the new highway
connects Nome with the Interior.

Nome is in Eskimo country, and much of its population is now

A pool deep in the mountains

Eskimo. You can see native craftsmen in some of the Nome shops and in the co-operative of Eskimo women, the Nome Skin Sewers. You can walk on Front Street to an Eskimo village where the King Islanders come every summer to set up temporary tent homes and where you can sometimes see them carve ivory or perform in native dances.

Not too far from Nome are a number of Eskimo villages, Kotzebue, Unalakleet, Shishmaref. Far to the north, at the northernmost point in Alaska on the Arctic Ocean, is Barrow, probably the largest Eskimo village in the world, with a population of 1,200. The Eskimos at Barrow still stalk polar bears on the Arctic ice only a few miles from the Navy's Arctic Research Laboratory. Here in the Arctic are the most haunting contrasts between old and new;

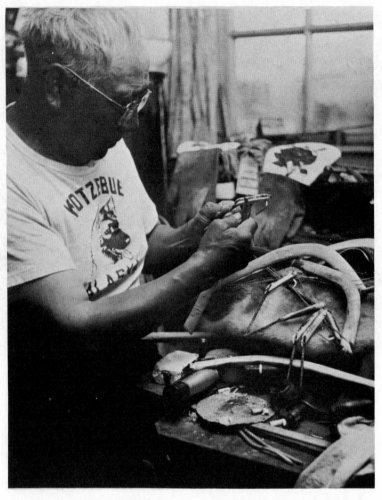

An Eskimo ivory carver in Kotzebue

modern airplane facilities and whale hunts, complex radar installations for defense and Eskimo women slaughtering seals just as
they have done for hundreds of years. Here are dog-sleds and
mechanized umiaks, traditional dances with the magic of ancient

A typical old Eskimo who waits to greet the visitor to Kotzebue

religions and teen-age bobby-soxers listening to battery-powered radios and phonographs blare out the latest "rock and roll" tunes. Here some natives have achieved prosperity on military jobs, while many still eke out a meager existence in the face of a hostile environment.

Thousands of visitors are drawn to Alaska primarily by its scenic grandeur and wild life rather than its historic or picturesque towns. For them Mount McKinley National Park offers the opportunity to see the untamed Alaska from the vantage point either of a luxury hotel or a well-kept camping ground. The great peak of Mount McKinley overshadows the entire park and the flat plain for hundreds of miles around. Here are remnants of the ice age, huge polished boulders high on the mountains where they were once car-

Boating at Camp Denali with Mount McKinley in the background

ried by glaciers which have long receded. And here out of the thin layer of top soil, above the permafrost which underlays most of the Interior, grow many types of willow, white spruce with dark green foliage and tawny cones, dwarf birch, their leaves dull green in summer but flaming scarlet at the first touch of frost.

Wild flowers abound in the park, blue lupine, asters, yellow cinquefoil, blue larkspur, fireweed, mountain azalea, tiny dryas matting the tundra with their oak-shaped evergreen leaves and creamy white flowers. In the park are 122 kinds of birds and 35 kinds of animals. In fact, it is possible to see here most of Alaska's wild life without need for extensive travel.

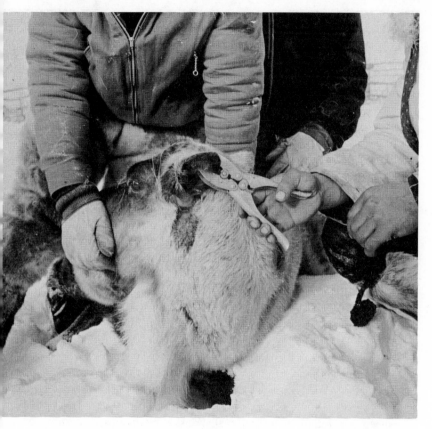

An aluminum tag is punched into the ear of government-owned deer,
a less painful method of identification than branding

Thousands of caribou, both the bulls and the cows with antlers,
move through the park in July on the way to their summer ranges.
The Dall Mountain Sheep, their coats snow-white and the rams with
long curled horns, remain on the mountainsides. The moose, biggest of the deer family, with bulls sometimes weighing up to 1,500
pounds, usually shun the open tundra but sometimes come out to
eat or water themselves at pools and lakes.

These three are among Alaska's favorite game animals, although
they cannot, of course, be shot in the park. The nimble mountain

A northern coyote in Mount McKinley National Park

sheep are found in virtually all Alaska mountains, but most of them are in the remote Brooks Range far to the north. Hunting is limited to the older rams, but it is these that provide the choicest trophy heads. There used to be so many caribou that paddle-wheel steamers were held up for hours on the Yukon while the herds crossed. Now the caribou are scarce, and are hunted both for trophies and meat. The moose are the most abundant of the game animals, and during the hunting season their horns are seen almost everywhere in Alaska, on autos and mounted over doors. The big Kenai Moose Range has been set up to protect them from extinction.

Bear of many kinds are common in Alaska, particularly the

Prize trophy—a big Kodiak bear

small black bear. Historic Kodiak Island, site of the first Russian settlement in Alaska, attracts many hunters in search of the Kodiak brown bear, the largest meat-eating animals in the world, running up to 1,600 pounds in weight. The big brown bear and the related but smaller grizzly are found also on Admiralty, Baranof, and Chichagof Islands and on the Alaska Peninsula. The huge white polar bear can be found in the Arctic, and one of the more dangerous sports is hunting them along the southern border of the Arctic ice peak. Polar bear skins fetch a good price, and some are exported every year.

Ptarmigan are the most widely distributed of Alaska game birds. They are found from southeast Alaska to the Arctic tundra. Hunt-

Seals on St. Paul Island, one of the Pribilof Islands

ers go after them with a small-bore shotgun requiring accurate shooting, much as they hunt quail. There are also several varieties of grouse, one of the most popular Alaska game birds.

There is excellent hunting out of Anchorage, Fairbanks, Kodiak Island, and the Kenai Peninsula. Fishing is good almost everywhere in Alaska. But southeast Alaska and the Katmai National Monument in Western Alaska, where there are several fine fishing camps, are especially famed for their king salmon fishing. Salmon derbies are conducted annually by a number of southeast towns.

The king salmon run from 20 to 40 pounds and are a prize catch. But the silver or coho salmon, less than half the weight, are considered a superior game fish. They fight the fishermen all the way, making fast runs downstream and then leaping into the air.

A rainbow trout taken at a fishing camp at Katmai National Monument

Alaska fishermen also go after red or sockeye salmon, pink or humpback salmon and chum or dog salmon. Fishing boats of all sizes and types are available at any southeast Alaska town.

Most abundant of Alaska's game fish are the grayling and the

A 65 pound 5 ounce prize winner

Dolly Varden trout. The grayling, very similar to the trout but distinguished by its big dorsal fin, is found in almost every important river north of the Gulf of Alaska. It has an insatiable appetite for flies, even coming clear out of the water to try for them.

Catching silver salmon and rainbow trout the easy way

It is a fighter, running downstream and then cross-current, thrashing up and down, in efforts to escape the inevitable. Excellent eating, the grayling runs to 23 inches and weighs up to 4½ pounds. The Dolly, running up to 30 inches, is a controversial creature.

Some fishermen despise it as lacking fight. Others hotly deny this, and say it is fine eating to boot.

The cutthroat trout, considered one of Alaska's best game and food fishes, is found mainly in southeast Alaska. It gets its name from two red lines on its jaw. Rainbow trout are found mainly in coastal rivers and in some Interior rivers south of the Yukon. The steelhead run eight to ten pounds, but larger ones are sometimes caught. These abound in coastal streams.

Sportsmen out for something different might try the sheefish, which is common in northern Alaska rivers. It is also called *inconnu* —the unknown; and nothing else like it is known under the American flag. It is a cross between a white fish and a salmon, averaging 20 pounds but sometimes running up to 80 pounds. The sheefish make excellent eating and there is a good commercial market for them in Nome.

Some sportsmen head straight from Seattle to their favorite Alaska hunting or fishing grounds, just stopping off to change planes. Others combine sports with sight-seeing. Then, of course, thousands of visitors are not particularly interested either in moose or king salmon, but just want to look at Alaska and meet its people.

Alaska has enough variety to satisfy almost everybody. It is a refuge for nature lovers armed only with cameras, for sportsmen with gun and rod, for tourists who want to see America's last frontier, for the restless and ambitious in search of opportunity. An Alaska in transition, striving to tame its wilderness and harness its resources, welcomes them all as it takes its place as the forty-ninth state in the Union.

Hints for Travelers

ABSENTEE OWNERS—outside investors in Alaska, especially the Alaska Steamship Company and the Seattle-owned canneries.

ABSENTEE GOVERNMENT—the control from Washington which prevailed prior to statehood.

ABSENTEE LABOR—refers to labor brought. in from the United States as well as to control by labor unions from the outside.

BELUGA—the 18-to-20-foot white whale used by the Eskimos as an important item of food.

CHEECHAKO—a newcomer or tenderfoot.

COSSACK—Eskimo slang for white man, a Russian hang-over.

HOOTCHENOO—the Indian homebrew, origin of the American slang expression, hootch.

IGLOO—an Eskimo dwelling of sod and timber, definitely not made of iceblocks.

IRON CHINK—an automatic device for splitting and cleaning fish in a cannery, replacing Chinese workers.

KAYAK—an Eskimo single passenger boat.

MALEMUTE—a sled dog.

MUKLUK—An Eskimo fur boot.

MUSH—move! an Indian version of the French *marche*.

OOGRUK—a large variety of seal used by Eskimos for food and clothing.

OUTSIDE—the United States. An Alaskan taking a trip to Seattle, for example, says he is going outside. Statehood may make this one obsolete.

PARKA—a warm Eskimo jacket, usually made of fur (pronounced "parky" in Alaska).

PERMAFROST—permanently frozen ground beneath the top layer of soil which thaws in spring.

POKE—a sealskin bag used for storing blubber; also refers to the moosehide bags used by the sourdoughs for gold dust. Poke can, therefore, also mean roll of wealth.

SIWASH—a contemptuous term for Indian or native, from the French *sauvage*.

SOURDOUGH—an old-timer, after the fermented dough used by the old-timers who didn't have yeast. A derisive variation is sour on Alaska, no dough to go outside.

TUNDRA—the swampy, rolling plains which cover much of the Interior and the Arctic in Alaska.

UMIAK—a large Eskimo skin boat.

A FEW BOOKS ON ALASKA

These are suggested for those who would like to do further reading on Alaska. It is very far from a complete list of even the better books on Alaska. Thousands have been published.

Guide Books

Guide to Alaska—$2, Box 1204, Cathedral City, California. A handy book with helpful information for tourists.

The Mile Post—$1.25, Box 457, Cathedral City, California. Indispensable for motorists coming over the Alaska Highway; has useful maps.

A Guide to Alaska—by Merle Colby. Macmillan. This book, prepared under the auspices of the WPA Federal Writers Project, was published in 1939, and is now outdated as a practical guide. But it is worth getting out of the library for fascinating lore and background information.

History

The State of Alaska—by Ernest Gruening. Random House. $7.50. Somewhat expensive and detailed for the general reader, this book by a former governor and now United States Senator from Alaska is the best in the field, especially on the American period in Alaska, on Alaska's economic problems, and on the fight for statehood.

Alaska—by Stuart Tomkins. University of Oklahoma Press. $4. A good general history of Alaska, with emphasis on the Russian period.

Road to Alaska—by Douglas Coe. Julian Messner. $2.50. The epic story of the Alaska Highway.

Old Yukon Tales, Trails and Trials—by James Wickersham. Washington Law Book Co. You'll have to get this one out of the library, but it has wonderful true stories of the Gold Rush, the Klondike, Nome and Alaska justice in the old days. It is written by the man Alaskans consider the father of statehood.

Lord of Alaska—by Hector Chevigny. The Viking Press. $3.50. A dramatic biography of Alexander Baranof, the man who built the Russian empire in America.

General Information

Mid-Century Alaska—Government Printing Office. $1. A good handbook of general information on Alaska compiled by the Department of the Interior.

Alaska: 1958–1959—Government Printing Office. 20 cents. An up-to-date pamphlet of general information issued by the Department of the Interior.

Alaska: The Land and the People—by Evelyn I. Butler and George A. Dale. Viking. $3.50. The authors, for many years educators among the native peoples in Alaska, give an intimate account of Eskimo and Indian life today as well as a general picture of Alaska. Written for teenagers, the book is useful for all age groups.

Adventure and Exploration

The Friendly Arctic—by Vilhjalmur Stefansson. Macmillan. $6. One of the best and most exciting accounts of polar exploration. Stefansson's new ideas and theories about the Arctic aroused a major controversy.

My Life with the Eskimos—by Vilhjalmur Stefansson. Macmillan. $7. A fascinating account of life in the Arctic with much valuable information about the Eskimos.

Mush, You Malemute—by Bernard R. Hubbard, S. J. The glacier priest tells the story of his adventures in Alaska.

Fiction and Poetry

The Spoilers—by Rex Beach. Story of the attempt by claim-jumpers in Nome to rob the discoverers of gold.

The Silver Horde—by Rex Beach. The story of how the salmon trust tried to bar gold miners and competitive canneries and clashed with them.

The Iron Trail—by Rex Beach. The struggle between rival interests to build the first railroad in Alaska.

Burning Daylight—by Jack London. A prospector strikes it rich, becomes a financial tycoon in California, then decides he doesn't want his wealth after all.

The Spell of the Yukon—by Robert Service. Dodd, Mead & Co. $2. This volume contains some of Service's famous ballads of the gold rush days, including "The Shooting of Dan McGrew" and "The Cremation of Sam McGee."

TRANSPORTATION AND TOURS

Airlines: Four airlines offer service from Seattle to Alaska. These are Alaska Airlines, Northwest Orient Airlines, Pacific Northern Airlines, and Pan American World Airways. Northwest Orient also offers daily flights to Alaska from New York via Seattle (2½ hr. stopover) and once a week flights (Fridays) from Minneapolis; they also have a flight to Anchorage via Edmonton, Canada. Approximate one-way fares without tax from Seattle are $49 to Ketchikan, $55 to Juneau, $75 to Anchorage, $90 to Fairbanks.

Airlines offering service inside Alaska include Alaska Airlines, Alaska Coastal Airlines, Cordova Airlines, Ellis Airlines, Northern Consolidated Airlines, Pacific Northern Airlines, Pan American World Airways, Reeve Aleutian Airways, and Wien Alaska Airlines.

Steamship: Alaska Cruise Lines Ltd., 420 Vance Building, Seattle, Washington, operates S.S. *Glacier Queen* and S.S. *Chilcotin* from early June through early September from Vancouver to Skagway through the inside passage. Eight-day round-trip fares range from $195 to $295 during early June and $245 to $330 after that. Canadian National Steamships, 214 Vance Building, Seattle, operates the S.S. *Prince George* from late May through September 6 from Vancouver to Skagway. Round-trip fares for nine days range from $235 to $507.50. Canadian Pacific, White-Henry-Stuart Building, Seattle, has sailings on the S.S. *Princess Louise* from Vancouver to Skagway for a minimum fare of $215. One-way trips are also available.

Auto: Allow yourself six to eight days for the 2,440-mile drive between Seattle and Fairbanks. It is about 100 miles more if you start at Spokane east of the Cascades and about 30 miles less if you begin the trip from Great Falls. The first part of the trip is over the historic Cariboo Trail which connects with the Hart Highway, a short cut making the distance several hundred miles less than in past years. The Alaska Highway proper starts at Dawson Creek, British Columbia, and stretches 1,523 miles to Fairbanks. Considerable sections of the highway in Canada are unpaved and get dusty in the summer. It is wise to cover the gasoline tank with rubber tubing against gravel, and to take extra gas and a basic set of car tools. Speed should be limited to about 40 miles an hour. Allow about 50 cents a gallon for gasoline. There are lodges and service stations spaced along the road at an average of about 30 miles each. Expenses along the road, including the gasoline, lodging and food, come to about $30 a day for two persons. In planning a trip by car consult *The Mile Post,* and *Alaska: 1958–1959,* listed herein under "A Few Books on Alaska."

Canadian Customs Requirements: While passports are not required for United States citizens entering Canada, identification papers are extremely helpful. Naturalized citizens should take certifications of naturalization. Travelers entering Canada by auto are required to show that they have sufficient funds for the trip. If their cars are old or in poor condition, they will need a Commercial Vehicle Permit with a cash deposit or bond for export. Trailers may be barred in Canada if the automobiles hauling them are considered too light. Tourists planning to drive to Alaska should write to the Canadian Government Travel Bureau, Ottawa, Canada, for entrance requirements and customs regulations.

Tours: Tours of Alaska are offered by the following agencies:
Arctic Alaska Tours, 420 Vance Building, Seattle, Washington.
American Express Company, 65 Broadway, New York, New York.
Scenery Unlimited Tours, 2123 Addison St., Berkeley, California.
Thomas Cook & Son, 587 Fifth Ave., New York, New York.
Brownell Tours, Brownell Building, Birmingham, Alabama.
Greyhound Highway Tours, 741 Market St., San Francisco 3, California.
Happiness Tours, 6 East Monroe Street, Chicago, Illinois.

Airlines offering tours:

Alaska Airlines, 1309 Fourth Ave., Seattle 9, Washington.
Canadian Pacific Airlines, Vancouver, B.C., or any CPA office.
Cordova Airlines, Box 1499, Anchorage, Alaska.
Northwest Orient Airlines, White-Henry-Stuart Building, Seattle, Washington.
Northern Consolidated Airlines, International Airport, Anchorage, Alaska.
Pacific Northern Airlines, 1233 Fourth Ave., Seattle, Washington.
Pan American World Airways, Seattle-Tacoma Airport, Seattle, Washington, or any district sales office.
Reeve Aleutian Airways, Box 559, Anchorage, Alaska.
United Airlines, 4th and University, Seattle, Washington, or any district sales office.
Wien Alaska Airlines, Fairbanks, Alaska.

Special tours:

NEA Tours, Division of Travel Service, National Education Association, 1201 16th St., N.W., Washington, D.C., offers tours for the field of education.

Thru the Lens Tours, 4344 Laurel Canyon Blvd., Studio City, California, has tours for camera fans.

A few sample tours from early June through early September:

Arctic Alaska Tours offers a Golden Belt Line cruise, a 16-day tour which includes a cruise of the inside passage, a motor trip by bus from White Horse to Fairbanks, a tour of Mount McKinley National Park, a visit to the Anchorage area and a return to Seattle by plane for $495 plus tax in the thrift season (before early June) and a regular rate of $575 plus tax.

Arctic Alaska offers a 12-day Totem Special tour through the Inside passage with auto and railroad trips through old gold-mining trails for $320 plus tax.

Wien Alaska Airlines offers a three-day Arctic Coast tour to Nome and Kotzebue from Fairbanks for $155.50 plus tax.

Alaska Airlines offers a ten-day tour which includes extensive air travel inside Alaska plus a Tanana River cruise and a rail trip to Mount McKinley National Park for $359 plus tax.

HOTELS, LODGES, AND MOTELS

Hotel accommodations in Alaska range from very modern to survivals from pioneer days. There are a few fine hotels that rate first-class by any standards. New motels are rapidly being built. There are also old-time roadside inns called "roadhouses" that date from the dog-mushing days. Most of these have been modernized enough to include electric lights and indoor plumbing. What follows is a list of hotels, road accommodations and lodges compiled by the Alaska Visitors Association. Where rates are listed, they were provided to AVA in response to a questionnaire in 1958:

Anchorage

Anchorage Hotel, Box 360. 100 rooms, modern, with and without baths.

Anchorage Inn. Twins with bath, $14 double.

Chitty's Motel, Box 992, Mt. View Branch. 12 rooms w/bath; 7 w/o; $8 up; kitchenettes available.

Hope Vacation Ranch, Box 2202.

Lane Hotel, Box 246. Rooms with and without bath.

North Star Motel, 14330 Gambell St. 25 rooms all with bath, modern, cafe attached.

Palace Hotel, Box 1287.

Parsons Hotel, 300 H St.

Roosevelt Hotel, 539 H St. 40 rooms, none with bath, second class; singles, $3–$6; doubles $5–$8.

Spring Creek Lodge, Star Route.

Travelers Inn, 720 Gambell St. 52 units, dining room and cocktail lounge, modern; $14 up.

Westward Hotel, Third & F Sts. 115 rooms with bath, $8.50–$12; 25 without bath, $5–$9; double or twin with bath. $12–$16; new dining room; no charge for children.

Westward Inn, Fifth Avenue & Gambell Sts. 28 rooms with bath, single $9, double $15; no charge for children; modern.

Aniak

Aniak Lodge, Box 26. Fishing—salmon, trout, pike, grayling, white-fish, and shee.

Bell Island Hot Springs

Bell Island Health Springs Resort. Operates year-round; 5 rooms with bath, $8–$10; 7 w/o bath, $5–$7; no charge for children under 5 yrs., all cabins furnished for housekeeping; dining room. Cocktail lounge and general store. Boats, motors, fishing tackle, gas and oil.

Big Delta

Bays Hotel. Modern log structure, dining room.

Buffalo Lodge.

Chamberlain's Hotel.

Chitina

Chitina Hotel.

Tebay Lakes Fishing Camp. Open May-Sept., good fishing.

Circle Hot Springs

Circle Hot Springs Hotel and Cabins, via Fairbanks. Reservations through Wien Alaska Airlines, Fairbanks. Indoor and outdoor pools.

Copper Center

Copper Center Lodge. $4 per person.

Cordova

Cordova Hotel and Bar.

Northern Hotel. Rooms with and without bath. Apts., housekeeping, one or two rooms from $60 to $90 mo.

Windsor Hotel. Singles and doubles with and without bath. Rates by week or month, available "off-season."

Milepost 1361 Dot Lake

Dot Lake Lodge. Lodge, cabins, and house trailers. No bath. Modern.

Excursion Inlet via Juneau

Tongass Lodge. (American Plan) $18 a day, couples $34, 10% off for weekly stays.

Fairbanks

Alaska Apt. Motel. $12 double.

Alaska Inn, 419 Fourth.

Aurora Lodge, 39 Mile Richardson Highway. 14 rooms available in May, with and without baths. Building extension. Will have gen. merch., sporting goods, and grocery store.

Birch Tree Trailer Court, 613 Twenty-second.

Fairbanks Hotel, $6–$10.

Fifth Avenue Hotel, 637 Fifth Ave. 29 rooms without bath.

Lacey St. Hotel, 501 Third Ave.

Nordale Hotel, $8.50–$14.

Northhaven Tourist Court, Box 226, College, Alaska. Log cabins, all cooking facilities furnished. Without bath.

Tanana Court. $6 per person.

Tamarac Inn Motel, Slaterville, Fairbanks. $6–$12.

Traveler's Inn, 820 Noble. 70 rooms with bath, cocktail lounge, banquet room.

Ft. Greeley Lodge. Delta Jct. south of Fairbanks. 7 rooms without bath. Tours of glaciers, mountains, fishing, hunting, etc. Garage service, towing, repairs.

Silver Fox Lodge. Mile 50 Richardson Hwy. (50 miles south of Fairbanks). Log construction with fireplace, rooms and cabins. Good moose hunting and grayling fishing. Tires, gas, oil, batteries, etc. available. Boats to rent nearby, skiing, swimming, etc.

Summit Lake Lodge. Mile 195 Richardson Hwy. Cabins, trailer court. Open in June for fishing season—trout, grayling. Hunting season opens August—sheep, and September for moose, caribou, and bear. Fishing tackle, boats, motors, gas, and oil available. Bar and restaurant. Closes September.

Chena Hot Springs Resort.

Wickersham Hotel.

Fort Yukon

Melville's Roadhouse, Box R, Ft. Yukon. Outside cabins (2–3 bedrooms). Water is a luxury, has to be boiled. Model A transp. in summer, dog team in winter.

Gakona

Hufman's Fishing & Hunting Camp, Paxson Lake P.O. Camp opens June 15, closes September 15. Housekeeping cabins, boats and motors. Fishing tackle, licenses. Hunting in season. Trips are arranged, guide service available.

Haines

Gateway Hotel, Lynn Canal Hotel Corp. New, modern, have 8 rooms, 4 with priv. bath, 4 with connecting bath, $7 up.

Hotel Halsingland, Box 158. First class; accommodate 125. Meals.

Schnabel Apt. Hotel. 14 rooms, with bath.

Homer

Baycrest Hotel (and Porpoise Room). 12 rooms, all with bath and h.w. heat. Dining room, cocktail bar.

Heady Hotel. $3.50 basement rooms without bath; $4; $4.50; $5 and $6 with bath single; $9 with bath double. Also dormitory.

Inlet Inn. Box 8. Waterfront location. $5 to $8 with or without bath.

King's Kabin Kourt, Box 72-A.

Seafair Motel. Rates: $6 and $8 with bath, h.w. heat, kitchenettes, fully modern.

Sewell Motel, Box 262. Rates with bath $8 and $10, h.w. heat, showers, kitchenettes.

Willards Moose Camp, Caribou Lake. Contact PNA agent, Homer, for reservations. Accessible only by air via PNA. Rates: $10 a day, log cabins, incl. meals, family style. Boats, motors, saddle horses.

Juneau

The Baranof Hotel, Second & Franklin St. 130 rooms with bath, $10–$25, family room to accom. 5, $22. Modern, bar, coffee shop.

Franklin Hotel.

Gastineau Hotel, P.O. Box 1601. 98 rooms. Rates: $4 and $6; doubles, $4, $6 and up, with and without baths. Modern.

Home Hotel.

Juneau Hotel, 104 Third St. Single $4 without bath; $5 with bath. Double $6 without bath, $8 with bath.

Taku Lodge. $20 a day (American Plan).

Tongass Lodge, Excursion Inlet. $18 a day (American Plan).

Kasilof

Pollard's Tongass Lodge. 4 rooms with bath. Regist. guide service for big game hunting. Pack and saddle horses. Boats. Cabins and dormitory. River-boat trips.

Kenai

Miller's Lodge, Box 139. Cabins and dormitory, cafe, picnic tables.

Ketchikan

Gilmore Hotel, 326 Front St. Operated in conjunction with Stedman Hotel. 42 rooms. Concrete, steam heated bldg. Telephone service each room. With or without bath.

Ingersoll Hotel. 55 rooms with bath, $8; 5 without bath, $5.50. Modern.

Stedman Hotel, 3009 Dock St., Box 319. Modern. 45 rooms with phone service. With or without bath. Coffee shop, cocktail bar. Rates: $4 to $7.50 and up.

Thayer Lake Lodge, Box 416. (On Admiralty Island.)

King Salmon, Bristol Bay

Air Martel. Reservations through airline agents. Rates: $4.50–$5.00, none with bath; dormitory, $3.50. Sports fishermen parties.

Kodiak

Kodiak Hotel. Rates: $5–$9.

Kotzebue

Wien Hotel, for Wien tourists.

Rotman's Hotel. Modern; $7; dining room.

Hanson's Trading Post. $4.

McKinley Park

McKinley Park Hotel. Season: June 8-September 8. Rates: $10 to $24 with bath, $8 to $16 without bath. Gift shop, cocktail lounge, dancing, tours, tennis, hiking. Car charter with driver.

Camp Denali. Lodge and camping facilities.

Moose Pass

Our Point of View Lodge, Kenai Lake, 5 rooms without bath, $6.50.

Nenana

Tortella Inn.

Ninilchik

Inlet View Cabins & Cafe, Mile 137.4, Starling Highway. 9 rooms without bath, $5 to $10. Good fishing and hunting with guide service available.

Nome
Polaris Hotel, Box 399. Rates: $5 to $12; special winter rates. Cocktail lounge.
Wallace Hotel, Box 56.
North Star Hotel. Modern, cafe.

Palmer
Hyland Hotel.
Matanuska Hotel. 42 rooms with bath, modern. Rates: $6 to $12.

Mile 110 Glenn Highway via Palmer
Meekins Lodge. Cabins and rooms. Facilities for fishing and hunting parties. Horses, boats, guides, also plane transportation on hunts. Reservations must be in by May 15.
Atlasta House, Glenn Highway. 5 rooms without bath. Rustic, comfortable. Hunting, fishing, hiking trails.
Sheep Mountain Lodge, Mile 113, Glenn Highway. Modern lodge. Steam heating system, with or without bath.

Petersburg
Mitkof Hotel, Box 1064. 10 rooms with bath, 24 without bath. Charges for children.

Seward
Murphy's Hotel.
New Seward Hotel, 217 Fifth, Box 246. Modern. 50 rooms $5 to $14, with and without bath. Charges made for children. Available: boats to rent, fishing and hunting.
Renrald Hotel. $3.

Mile 25, Seward Highway
Vacation Villa Motel. Semi-modern. 3 rooms without bath. Rates: $6 and up. Available: Deep-sea fishing excursions, gift shop, souvenirs.

Sitka
Sitka Hotel.

Skagway
Golden North Hotel. $8 single.
Skagway Inn. Capacity 24, rates: $3.50 and up.
Pullen House Annex. 6 double rooms. $3.50 up.
The Pullen House, Sixth & Spring. $6 and $8.
Pack Train Inn.

Sterling Kenai Peninsula

Bing Brown's Fishing Service. Rates: $2 to $7, with or without bath. Family style meals. Fishing trips (bring own equipment); rainbow trout up to 19 lbs. Also salmon.

Pedersen's Moose River Cabins. Located at junction of Moose and Kenai rivers. Daily and weekly rates, boats and motors for rent. Trailer court and campground.

Tok

Tok Lodge.

Parker House, Tok Junction. Modern. 3 rooms with bath, $12; 8 rooms without bath, $8 double. Dining room, family accommodations arranged.

Valdez

Valdez Hotel, Box 205. On the Square Town Center. Modern. 28 rooms with bath, 20 rooms without bath. Rates: $5 to $10.

Beals Hotel. 9 rooms without bath, but bath facilities available.

Alaskan Hotel. Can accommodate 27 guests, no rooms with bath but ample bath facilities on each floor. Rates: $3 to $5.

Port Valdez Motel. 6 units, $8–$10 a unit, each sleeping max. 6 persons. Shower and toilet in each unit. Double or twin beds plus rollaway beds if needed.

Wasilla

Big Lake Lodge, Star Route C.

Williwaw Lodge.

Wrangell

Gartley House. Rates: $4 a day, without private bath.

Glenn Highway lodges

Johnson Motel, Mile 15, The Town House. Cabins with kitchenette, with and without bath. Rates: $5 and $7. Weekly and monthly rates. Can raise husky dogs.

Sheep Mt. Lodge, Mile 113, G.H., Box 1732, Palmer. Cocktail bar, lounge with fireplace, home-cooked meals. Hunting, fishing, and winter sports. Rates: $4 and up, showers available. Weekly rates.

Spring Creek Lodge, Mile 20, G.H., Star Route, Anchorage. Only one cabin, not modern, but primarily restaurant and fountain lunch. Rates: $3 and $5 without bath.

Tazlina Glacier Lodge, Mile 156, G.H. Cabins, bunkhouse. Separate bathhouses for men and women, hot and cold showers. Rates: Single $2, bunkhouse; cabins $5 and $7.

Alaska Highway
Riverside Lodge, Mile 1283, Northway A.H. Rates: $4 to $10, with or without bath. Special rates by week or month.
Scottie Creek Lodge, Mile 1226. $4, $8, 26 rooms.
Beaver Creek Lodge. $4, $8.

Whitehorse, Y.T.
Whitehorse Inn. $5–$7 single; $8–12, double.
Taku Hotel. $8–$13 (new).
Regina Hotel. $3.50–$4.50.

HUNTING AND FISHING

Regulations on hunting and fishing and a list of guides can be obtained from the Alaska Game Commission or the Fish and Wild Life Service, Juneau, Alaska. Hunting and fishing booklets may also be obtained from these airlines:
Pan American World Airways, any district office.
Pacific Northern Airlines, 1233 Fourth Ave., Seattle, Washington.
Alaska Airlines, 2320 Sixth Ave., Seattle, Washington.
Northern Consolidated Airlines, Anchorage International Airport.

The hunting season is generally from August 20 to October 20, varying with the area and species. For nonresidents, a federal license fee of $50 and an Alaska fee of $8 covers all hunting, fishing, and trapping. A nonresident federal fishing license costs $2.50 and an Alaska fishing license is an additional $4, although a special 7-day fishing license may be obtained for $2.

Guides: Guide associations which may be contacted for further information include:
Alaska Guides Association, Box 1471, Anchorage.
Kodiak Guides Association, Kodiak.

A partial list of guides compiled by the Alaska Visitors Association follows:
Alaskan Air Adventures. Snowshoe Lake, Mile No. 147, Glenn Bay, Palmer, Alaska. Big-game hunting and fishing. Season, March through November. Sportsmen arriving in Alaska via air or ship will be met at Anchorage. Summer vacation camping, boats, and motors. Write above for further details.
Theodore J. Almasy, Registered Alaska Guide. McGrath, Alaska. Offers only personally conducted services to individuals and small parties. Fishing and hunting.

R. E. Betz. Box 4873, Spenard, Alaska. Bear, moose, caribou hunts. Fishing. Write for further details.

Arctic Hunts. Point Barrow, Alaska. Polar bear, caribou, spotted seal, and other game. Write for folders.

Ed Bilderback. Cordova, Alaska. Big-game hunting. Hunts include food, lodging, cook, and guides. Write for detailed information.

Carroll & Thompson. Box 485, Anchorage, Alaska. Pilots, guides, outfitters. Bear, sheep, caribou, wolf, moose.

Keith E. Hursch. P.O. Box 257, Kenai, Alaska. Season May to November. Bear, moose, caribou. Equipment furnished. Fishing equipment not furnished. Aircraft transportation. Write for details.

Marcus F. Jensen. 1012 2nd St., Douglas, Alaska. Experienced guide—black, brown bear, and moose. Trout fishing. Write for details.

Karl E. Lane. Box 1509, Juneau, Alaska. Guide and outfitter. Big-game and fishing. Equipment includes 36' cabin cruiser, canoes, skiff, outboards, etc. Summer charters for photographic and cruising ventures.

Alf Madsen. Kodiak, Alaska. Guide and outfitter, Kodiak Bear hunting, cruiser *Explorer;* camps.

Bill Poland. Guide and outfitter, Kodiak, Alaska. Hunting lodge 90 miles from Kodiak. Cruiser *Katmai.* Season April through October. Write for folder.

O. H. Vogel & Associates. Stephan Lake Hunting Camps, 545 L St., Anchorage, Alaska. Have seven camps. Big-game hunts for polar, grizzly, moose, caribou, and goat.

Guy Waddell. Box 97-A, Homer, Alaska. All camping equipment, boats and charter airplanes. Twin Lakes and Alaska Peninsula, grizzly, moose, etc.

Hugh S. Watson. Box 63, Homer, Alaska. Guide and outfitter. Hunting trips. If writing for price estimate, furnish details on size of party, wants, and needs.

Hal Waugh. Skagway, Alaska. Big-game hunting.

Ralph Wooton. Box 613, Petersburg, Alaska. Season May to October. Big-game hunting (with 50-foot cruiser *Radar*), also duck hunting and fishing.

Fishing: Fishing resorts and facilities compiled by the Alaska Visitors Association include:

Clover Pass Resort, Ketchikan.

Henry Hunter. Homer Dock, Homer, Alaska. One-day salt water fishing trips, tackle furnished; $10 a day.

Katmai Fishing Trips. Some of Alaska's best fishing is in or near the Katmai National Monument on the Alaska Peninsula about 250 miles from Anchorage. The famous "Valley of 10,000 Smokes" is in this park. Visitors from the East and Midwest can make arrangements through the Northwest Orient Airlines. Western sportsmen can contact the Northern Consolidated Airlines. Travel agencies can also furnish information.

Alf Madsen. Kodiak, Alaska. Complete fishing excursions, everything provided, $50 a day includes transportation. Fishing cruise on *Explorer* to Uganik Bay camp. Write for further information.

Tebay Fishing Camps. Jo Wilson, Chitina, Alaska. Flights in small aircraft to the Tebay lakes. Good fishing.

Charter Boats: The Alaska Visitors Association provides this list for sportsmen seeking to charter boats:

R. M. Bernhoft. c/o Tongass Trading Co., Ketchikan. Yacht *Swiftsure.* Hunting, fishing, sightseeing. Write for further information.

Ed Bilderback, Cordova, Alaska. MV *Valiant Maid.* Capacity nine persons. $130 a day.

Roy Connors. 347 Irwin St., Juneau.

J. M. Coon. Ketchikan, Alaska. Yacht *Manana II.*

Bill Ray. 206 Franklin St., Juneau, Alaska.

Chuck 'n Bob's Charter Service. 127 Behrends Ave., Juneau, Alaska. Phones 6–1471 and 6–2717. 28′ twin screw cabin cruiser. Available for salmon fishing or sightseeing.

CALENDAR OF ALASKA EVENTS

January

Polar bear hunting in the Arctic. Continues through April.
Skiing. Continues through March.
Nome—Crabbing.
Cordova—Annual Masquerade Ball.
Tox, Kotzebue and other villages—Dog-team Races.
Palmer—Ice Fishing on nearby lakes.

February

Anchorage—Annual Fur Rendezvous.
Fairbanks—Skiing weekends and holidays on Cleary Summit.
Juneau—Gold Medal basketball tournament.

March

Fairbanks—Ice Carnival. Dog-team Races. Snowshoe baseball game.
Juneau—Annual Arts and Crafts Show. Southeast Alaska Ski Championship.
Kotzebue—Spring Festival, dog races.
Homer—Ice Carnival.

Ketchikan—Season-long Salmon Derby begins in early March.
Nenana—Dog-team races.

April

Juneau—Juneau Boat Show.
Cordova—Razor Clam Digging.
Nenana—Tanana River ice break-up April or May.

May

Palmer—Colony Days in commemoration of founding of agricultural colony in late May around Memorial Day.
Valdez—Fish for Fun Derby, May to August.
Petersburg—Norwegian Independence Day Celebration, singing, dancing, folk dancing, fish fry. Mid-May.
Cordova—White King Salmon fishing.

June

Anchorage—Annual Music Festival.
Fairbanks—Midnight Baseball Game.
Chugiak—Annual Carnival.
Ketchikan—Two-day Salmon Derby, early in June.
Skagway—Days of '98 Show, every boat night.
Petersburg—Saint Hans Day Midsummer Celebration.
Haines—Strawberry Festival, late June and early July.

July

Fairbanks—Golden Days.
Valdez—Outboard Races, early July.
Nenana—Fairbanks-Nenana Boat Marathon.
Point Barrow—Whalefest when first whale is caught.
Anchorage—Lake George break-up between July 15 and August 1.
Skagway—Days of '98 Show, every boat arrival night.
Sitka—Annual Salmon Derby.
Juneau—Golden North Salmon Derby.
Fourth of July Celebrations nearly everywhere.

August

Hunting season opens.
Fairbanks—Tanana Valley Fair, mid-August.
Palmer—Matanuska Valley Fair, at end of August.
Valdez—Truck Road-eo.
Skagway—Harvest Fair, late August, also Days of '98 on boat nights.
Valdez—Silver Salmon Derby, whole month.
Juneau and Homer—4-H Fairs.

September

Cordova—Salmon Derby, usually Labor Day weekend.

4-H Fairs—late August and early September at Ninilchik, Galena, McGrath, Kaltag, Anvik, Anika, Slietmute, Mission, Kwethluk, Aliak, Minto, Fort Yukon, Circle, Beaver Venetie.

Anchorage—All Alaska 4-H Fair.

October

Sitka—Alaska Day, October 18. Pageant and Ceremonies commemorating the purchase of Alaska.

Bethel—Hallowe'en Dance.

December

Petersburg—Old Country Yulefest.